SOCIAL SKILLS SURVIVAL GUIDE

A HANDBOOK FOR INTERPERSONAL AND BUSINESS ETIQUETTE

JUNE HINES MOORE

BROADMAN
&HOLMAN
PUBLISHERS

NASHVILLE, TENNESSEE

0-8054-2633-7

Published by Broadman & Holman Publishers
Nashville, Tennessee

Dewey Decimal Classification: 395
Subject Heading: ETIQUETTE \ MANNERS AND CUSTOMS \
UNITED STATES–SOCIAL LIFE AND CUSTOMS

1 2 3 4 5 6 7 8 08 07 06 05 04 03

Dedication

I dedicate this book to my husband, Homer, my greatest inspiration; to our family; and to all the students I have had the privilege to teach in my twenty-year career.

We put etiquette rules in our head. We carry manners in our heart. Together they keep us from embarrassing others or ourselves.

Contents

Acknowledgments

I want to acknowledge and thank these fine young adults who were kind enough to share with me their valuable experiences, insights, and suggestions:

Tonda Nations, researcher with *FamilyLife Today*; Richard Smith, attorney-at-law; Kaylyn Hickey, former schoolteacher and now student at Dallas Theological Seminary; and Greg Moore, accountant and business owner.

My gratitude goes to Acquisitions Editor, Leonard Goss who granted permission to publish my book. A special thanks also goes to Kim Overcash, the project editor, who worked tirelessly on the manuscript, and who, as intermediary, went the extra mile for me.

Introduction

In technology today the click of a mouse or the touch of a key can take you where you want to be, but without good manners (effective interpersonal skills), you may not achieve your goals.

Manners and civility rooted in genuine caring are cornerstones in any great society, but it sometimes seems we are enduring an epidemic of rudeness. Ugly signs of wholesale "selfness" are all around us.

As reported in the Arkansas Democrat-Gazette (2 August 2001), a man at a restaurant busily clipped his nose hairs over breakfast. And, as a young speaker was addressing a civic club, another man was loudly clipping his nails over his half-eaten meal for all to see and hear.

Another story is told of a young woman patiently waiting in the refreshment line at the movie theater only to watch the kid behind the counter wait on three customers behind her before finally taking her order. Then her completed order was handed to the person standing behind her. Some people seem to go out of their way to be rude and thoughtless.

Dismissed in the past as elitism or snobbery, etiquette has made a comeback. With road rage, airport rage, and general outrage all around us, our society now seems to recognize the importance of civility and good old-fashioned manners. The tragic world-shaking events of September 11, 2001, have awakened in all of us a greater sense of patriotism and civility toward one another. The firefighters and policemen who died at Ground Zero gave their last full measure of kindness in trying to save the lives of those in the towers of the World Trade Center.

Through the information in this book, it is my hope that you will develop more confidence in yourself as you practice proper etiquette and good manners in your daily life.

Chapter 1

What Are Manners and Etiquette for Young Adults?

If you are like most young adults, there are probably times when you feel uncomfortable because you are unsure what is expected of you in social, formal, or business situations. Maybe you are not sure what to wear, how to introduce yourself, what to say after the introduction, which fork to use, how to conduct yourself in a job interview, or where to find the answer to other questions of proper conduct. Uncertainty can make you uneasy.

Occasionally even the best-intentioned person makes a *faux pas* (*fopah*, French for mistake; literally, "false step") by not knowing what to do or how to handle embarrassing moments. It's sometimes possible to fake it, to pretend that you know what you are doing. You can appear to be in control and have it all together, but faking it won't carry you very far. You may spend a lot of time worrying that you will be discovered because you don't have a clue what to say or do.

Compare that feeling to how you feel when you have studied hard and aced a test. You know when you have achieved success. Now that's real confidence, and the way to capture such self-assurance in social and business situations is to learn the rules of etiquette and why they are important. Learning the proper conduct gives you the knowledge you need. With the rules in your head and manners in your heart, you won't embarrass yourself or someone else. Together they will guide you and tell you how to act in every situation.

> *Manners are the happy way of doing things.*—Ralph Waldo Emerson

Manners and Etiquette

Manners are the kind expression of the principles of etiquette. That's why the rules of etiquette are kept in your head, and manners come from your heart. They aren't sold in stores, and they aren't given to you when you are born. Consideration for others' feelings and a courteous manner spring from the heart, from the desire to put others at ease, even in awkward or difficult situations.

> *The word* etiquette *is said to come from the idea of labels or stickers attached to things (and now people) proclaiming what they are and where they belong.*[1]
> —Margaret Visser, *The Rituals of Dinner*

> *The word* etiquette *is a French word that means "ticket." In the days of the French kings, the lords and nobles were given "etiquettes" to tell them to stay off the grass when they were not inside the Versailles Palace where Louis XIV held court sessions. Other tickets were given to them to show where they were to stand in court, representing their province (state).*

Manner means "a habit, a way of doing something." *Etiquette* means "the practice of correct behavior." Having good manners means using the principles of etiquette to show kindness from your caring attitude to others. When you say please and thank-you and when you open a door for someone, you are using good etiquette and good manners because you have a genuine desire to assist someone or be kind to them.

Self-confidence in presenting yourself well and treating others properly depends on a basic knowledge of the code of proper behavior. The traditions and practices of good manners answer the questions, what am I suppose to do, and when do I do it? During your lifetime additional rules may have to be written to accommodate new technology, but what you learn now about courtesy and good manners will never change. Confidence and poise come with the knowledge and use of good manners. You can't practice what you don't know, but with the right principles in your mind, you can shift the focus off yourself and onto the people around you. Life is a lot happier that way.

The Golden Rule

All etiquette comes from the original Golden Rule that Jesus gave us in Matthew 7:12: "Therefore, whatever you want others to do for you, do also the same for them." Manners were God's idea first, and often in the New Testament, Jesus speaks of treating people with kindness. In Philippians 2:3–4 Paul says, "Do nothing out of rivalry or conceit, but in humility consider others as more important than yourselves. Everyone should look out not only for his own interests, but also for the interests of others." Galatians 5:14b says, "Love your neighbor as yourself." When you practice the precepts of etiquette and have kind regard in your heart, you are living the Golden Rule and following God's command to love others.

> *Jesus participated in many social and religious rituals and objected to bad manners. He nevertheless condemned the false pretences to purity of soul which were expressed, for example, by pre-dinner ablutions, and pointed to Isaiah's insight that God detests "lip-service" that covers up the truth. Self-aggrandizing ritual was to be replaced by actions expressing real love and humility.[2]*
>
> —Margaret Visser, *The Rituals of Dinner*

Perhaps you were fortunate enough to have parents who taught you how to behave properly; but now you are on your own, and more is required of you as you are judged by each new situation. The only solution now is to learn what's expected of you wherever or with whomever you find yourself. Those bad table manners your parents may have overlooked in the past, may now embarrass you in front of friends or coworkers. You are expected to meet and make conversation with new acquaintances or business or college associates. Remember, etiquette is simply common sense and thoughtful behavior. It provides the guidelines for knowing how to act in almost every situation involving contact with other people. Proper etiquette is a bridge from your feeling of self-consciousness to a feeling of self-confidence.

> *The essence of good manners consists in freely pardoning the shortcomings of others although nowhere falling short yourself.*
>
> —Erasmus, 1530

Once you know how to make a good first impression, you can enter the world of confidence in making good impressions while leaving embarrassment, awkwardness, and fear behind you.

Chapter 2

First Impressions

You have probably heard it said that you never get a second chance to make a first impression. That hardly seems fair. After all, in tennis you get two chances to volley the ball over the net when you serve. And in amateur golf, if you bungle the first tee shot, you can hit the ball again and choose the better shot for your score. It's called a mulligan.

But in real life we may make first and lasting impressions many times daily. First impressions are formed within the first thirty seconds of an encounter with someone. How you interact with people can make or break your chances of being remembered well. Being well-groomed and attractively and appropriately dressed can go a long way toward making a good impression. Attire, grooming, demeanor, poise, and body language count when meeting people. If you are not sure what the appropriate clothing is for an occasion such as an interview, ask someone. A teacher or other more experienced adult should be able to help. (You'll find more information on proper attire in chapter 5, "Dressing to Achieve.")

Grooming

Grooming is how clean, neat, and tidy you appear. Body language is the message you give with your body and hands. Poise is the way you walk, sit, stand, and carry yourself. Together they show whether we are nervous, embarrassed, or uncomfortable. Image is the total package of grooming, poise, body language, and demeanor.

Body Language

We do it all the time. We move our hands around to supplement our speech. It's called gesturing or nonverbal communication. We flail. We point. We curl and uncurl our fingers. We wave. When we gesture, we give a "snapshot of our thinking, a window to our mind, the best way—without neurosurgery—of getting a peek inside the language center of our brain," according to David McNeill, professor of psychology and linguistics at the University of Chicago.

Professor McNeill's study of nonverbal communication showed that "At least half of language is imagery, and the gesture—the way we move our hands—plays out that image more spontaneously than the spoken words. . . . Gesture is a hand movement that is as much a part of language as speech. We create images with our hands."[1]

Other examples of gesturing are lifting arms, banging a fist into a palm, wiggling fingers, putting hands to eyes, and dropping our palms to our lap. The placement of our arms tells if we are angry or friendly. For instance, if you cross your arms across your chest with your hands tucked under your arms, you will look mad, cold, and unfriendly. However, if you cross your arms with your hands in plain sight, resting on top of your arms, you will have an open, friendly, approachable appearance.

Speech teachers and others have criticized gesturing as a substitute for finding the precise words and language to articulate what we want to say. Gesture can be good, and it can be bad. Even grade school children know some gestures that are never appropriate; however, moving the hands and arms to facilitate speech can be good.

Some of us are more prone to gesturing than others. Dr. McNeill says, "The more articulate and well-educated a person is, the more likely you are to see gesture."

Another way we reveal a glimpse into our psyche is what we do with our hands and arms when we are standing still. The best stance is with both arms hanging loosely at one's sides. A common, but incorrect gesture is when we hold our hands together below the waist, with arms straight, forming a V. This posture droops the shoulders and does not portray the best image for us. It's sometimes called the "fig leaf position." When we use it, we call attention to a private part of the body.

Women, but not men, can properly hold their hands together at their waist. Men and women can hold their hands behind their backs, but putting one's hands on the hips indicates anger or domination.

Demeanor

Demeanor is the expression on your face, your attitude. It can be friendly, surly, quiet, modest, indifferent, or aggressive.

Your demeanor is expressed on your face when you smile, frown, or scowl. Smiling comes naturally to some people but not to others; but everyone can develop the habit.

We all have the equipment to smile from birth, according to Dr. Susan Jones, an assistant professor of psychology at Indiana University who studies infants' smiles. Her research also shows that eighteen-month-old babies stop smiling when no one pays attention to them. Very young infants can tell the difference between a smiling and a frowning face. "And from about the age 10 months," Jones says, "babies look at facial expressions to get information about an ambiguous situation."

We continue this social referencing into adulthood. "If we are walking down the street and come across what seems to be a tense situation, we glance at other people to see from their expressions if it's a real emergency," Dr. Jones adds.[2]

With a confident demeanor, your goal can be a feeling of competence in presenting yourself so you can think of the needs and comfort of others instead of your own fears of embarrassment.

Poise

Poise is expressed in your posture, composure, aplomb, self-assurance, polish, gestures, and mannerisms. We sometimes call it body language. The way you stand, walk, and hold your arms says a lot about the way you feel about yourself.

To check your poise and posture, pretend you have one end of a string attached to your chest with the other end attached to the ceiling. Imagine someone pulling that string upward and see how you raise your torso upward. By doing so, you will straighten yourself without throwing your shoulders back and out of line. You will draw in your stomach and keep your head erect. The string technique will keep you from slouching or slumping. And it won't give you an unnatural, stiff appearance.

"The ramrod-straight military posture (Shoulders back!), long beloved by drill sergeants and admired by generations of parents and teachers, now seems laughably exaggerated. Not even the U.S. Military Academy at West Point, New York, encourages it anymore. The Point officially abandoned the so-called brace position in 1968 after an Army study showed it can cause a variety of medical problems."[3] When you walk with your head up, your arms swinging loosely by your sides, and as though you have a definite destination, you present yourself well. When you shuffle your feet or amble along aimlessly, you present yourself in a negative light.

Your actions, what you say to people, and how you say it, including your expressions, round out your chance to make a good first impression, your image.

Image

Grooming, attire, body language, poise, and demeanor all make up your overall image—the way you look, act, and express yourself. Image is your calling card; it's what you leave behind; it's what people remember about you. It all makes up the first and lasting impression you portray to others.

> *In 1997, a judge in New Orleans declared a mistrial in a case because the plaintiffs' lawyer was too charming. She found that "certain body language messages were conveyed."*
>
> *She also said, "It cannot be transcribed in a record, but the court is aware that he has a pleasant disposition and a charismatic personality. The rapport of the attorneys will not have a limited effect on the jury in this case."*
>
> —*The Associated Press,* 7 August 1997

Meeting and Greeting

People notice your outward appearance first, but they also notice what you say and how you act when they meet you. You need to know how to introduce yourself and others, as well as how to make small talk and polite conversation with new acquaintances and peers.

Greet everyone with a friendly smile. When it is appropriate, say, "Hello, how are you?"

> *A polite person is* polished *(from the French* poli*).*

Introducing Yourself with the Six Ss
- Stand
- Smile
- See their eyes
- Shake hands
- Speak your name
- Say their name back to them

Most of us have trouble with introductions, whether introducing ourselves or someone else. We have trouble remembering names, and we can't remember the rules. If you learn the six Ss and practice them often, you will always be comfortable when you meet people.

The first four Ss—stand, smile, see their eyes, and shake hands—are done almost simultaneously. The last two—speak your name and say the other person's name back to them—follow.

1. Stand. It's always polite to stand when you are meeting or greeting someone.

2. Smile. The smile is a language the deaf can hear and the blind can see. It takes fourteen muscles to smile and over seventy to frown.

3. See their eyes. Making eye contact with people is important. If you have trouble looking people in the eye, practice introducing yourself in front of a mirror. You will soon become more comfortable.

4. Shake hands. A handshake should be firm, but not crushing nor limp. The Protocol School in Washington teaches that the web between your thumb and index finger should meet the web of the other person's hand.[4] To keep your hand dry, wipe your hand on your clothing before extending it, if necessary. Don't pump someone's hand up and down as though you were priming a pump.

5. Speak your name. Say your name slowly and distinctly, giving your first and last name.

6. Say the person's name back to him or her. After you have introduced yourself to someone, and the person tells you his or her name, repeat the name saying, "Hello, Mr. Sails." Repeating a name helps you remember it and makes sure you understand it correctly. It also makes other people feel good when you say their name.

■■   ■■   ■■

A View of Manners from Bible Days

There are many examples in the Bible of meeting and greeting people. One is the story of God greeting Samuel for the first time by audibly calling out Samuel's name, and Samuel thought Eli was calling him. Samuel must have had a difficult time realizing that God was calling him.

Salutations in Bible Times

When travelers in the Middle East meet each other along the way, they engage in salutations that to a Westerner seem complicated, tedious, and time-consuming (not to mention nosy). Wordy questions will be asked seeking such information as this: From where have you come? Where are you going? What is your name? How many children have you? How many men belong to your clan? What enemies does your clan have? etc., etc. While such salutations are carried out, business and everything else can wait. For this reason, when Jesus sent the seventy disciples on a healing and preaching

mission, he said to them: 'Salute no man by the way'
(Luke 10:4). To engage in such extensive salutations as
were customary would have interfered with the urgent
business of the Lord.[5]

Chapter 3

Introducing Others

> *The most important rule for making introductions is to make the effort, even if you can't remember the names or forget the rules.*

Now that you can introduce yourself confidently and comfortably, using the six Ss, you need to learn the proper way to introduce your friends and acquaintances. Most people get introduction amnesia at times and have trouble making introductions because they fear they can't remember the names of the individuals or the rules about who to introduce to whom.

The rules are not difficult if you simply learn that in social circles you should defer to age and gender. Show respect by honoring the elderly over young people and the female over the male. You can do this by giving up your seat or by introducing people to friends. In business, we honor the individual who ranks the highest among others in the same company. And when introducing a client, the client is honored over your company associate, even over the CEO. For instance, "Mr. Client, this is Mr. Granger, our chief executive officer."

How many times have you walked up to a group of people, hoping to be introduced, and been ignored instead? It's an awkward feeling. Knowing how that feels should make you want to try harder to remember to introduce people.

The purpose of making introductions is to make people known to one another by name and to make guests feel welcome. Exchanging names and giving descriptive or interesting information about each person helps the new acquaintances to begin a conversation. To show respect, introduce the younger to the older and the male to the female.

Remember and practice these simple guidelines for making smooth introductions.

The Rules for Making Introductions

- Honor the female over the male by turning first to the female and giving her the male's name. "Sarah, this is John Bennett, my next-door neighbor. John, this is Sarah Brown, my coworker."
- Honor the older person (unless it's a family member) before the younger by turning first to the older person and giving him or her the other person's name. "Reverend Charmes, this is my roommate, Laura McGrew. Laura, this is Reverend Charmes, our pastor here at St. Luke's."
- Honor the dignitary or high-ranking individual before the one of a lesser position by turning first to the dignitary and giving him or her the name of the other person. "Governor Jones, I'd like you to meet Walker Abrams, our new clerk." There is no need for repetition here if Walker is close enough to have heard the governor's name and title.
- Always introduce a less prominent (honored) person to a more important person. In other words, the less important person's name is said last.

To honor the older and the female (the more important person), simply turn to them, say their name first, and give them the name and information about the other person.

"Mary, this is my brother, Sam Napier. Sam, this is Mary Alps, a friend from church." (Mary is the female, so her name is spoken first.)

"Mr. Badgett, (older person) this is my mom, Alice Napier. Mom, this is Mr. Badgett, my new boss in the shipping department." Usually, we present family members to outsiders, treating the outsider as a guest in our home.

"Governor Huckstable (dignitary), this is my brother, Sam Napier. Sam, Governor Huckstable." or, "Dr. Kender, this is my dad, Bob Napier. Dad, Dr. Kender is our new internist."

You may choose phrases other than "This is. . . ." You may simply say, "[Mrs. Smyth], I'd like to introduce. . ." or, "Please meet. . . ."

According to international diplomatic protocol, women are presented to ambassadors, ministers in charge of legations, chiefs of state, royalty, and dignitaries of the church. In other words, say, "Mr. Ambassador, this is Joan Early or (Mrs. Early), our new chef."

After you have been introduced, simply say hello or, "It's nice to meet you," and repeat the person's name. It helps you remember it.

Shaking Hands

- Two females shake hands the same as two males.
- A man or boy being introduced to a woman or girl shakes hands only if she offers her hand first. This rule applies in social situations only. In business, either the male or the female may extend his or her hand first.
- A gracious host or hostess greets everyone with a handshake.

Useful Tips

- Always give both first and last names when making introductions.
- Don't assume it's appropriate to call someone by his or her first name in responding to an introduction (for example, "Hello, John," may not be as appropriate as "Hello, Mr. Wright"). If you are in doubt about using someone's first name, use the last name until he or she asks you to use the first name.

After the Introduction

- When leaving someone you have just met, always say something such as, "I am glad to have met you," or, "It was nice meeting you."
- When introducing someone to a group of five or more friends, say, "I would like everyone to meet Jean Samples." Later each one in the group can introduce herself or himself to the one introduced to the group as a whole.
- If you feel uncomfortable making introductions, practice with a friend or family member.
- When no one offers to introduce you to others, wait for a pause in the conversation, use the six Ss, and introduce yourself. "Hello, I'm Ken Lassiter." Smile. Look into the eyes of one individual and extend your hand. Then repeat the new acquaintance's name when he or she gives it. If you do not understand someone's name, ask again. "I'm sorry. I didn't understand your name."
- If a male is wearing gloves, he removes the right one to shake hands. A female keeps her gloves on.

In Business

- In the business world, introduce your peers from another organization or business (if they are not customers) to your boss. "Mr. Boss, this is Hank Shield, my tennis partner."
- Introduce your boss to a customer by calling the customer's name first. "Mr. Customer, this is my boss, Dan Burton."

- Introduce same-level associates within your company to peers from another company. "Sam Smith, this is my coworker, Ann Fowler."
- Shake hands with the new acquaintance long enough to exchange greetings.
- If your name is mispronounced when you are introduced, kindly correct it. Simply say, "It's John Smith."

Forgotten Names

If you need to introduce someone whose name you cannot remember, try reintroducing yourself to him, hoping he will give you his name. Another tactic is simply to look at the person whose name you don't remember and say, "Come meet my friend Karen. I think you will like each other. Oh, and tell me your name again." Your friend may pick up the ball and introduce himself to Karen. Or you can say, "This is my friend, Karen Hartsell." Then pause and hope the friend will reply with his or her own name. But you may simply have to admit that your mind has gone blank. "I'm sorry, but I can't remember names today. You'll have to help me out."

If you cannot remember either person's name, be honest and up-front by saying, "I'm sorry. I forget my own name under pressure. Please help me out and introduce yourselves."

Finally, never ignore the effort to introduce people. We have a responsibility to see that our friends and acquaintances get to know one another. If you are in friendly surroundings and are seated next to strangers for a time, introduce yourself by looking at the person and saying, "Hello. I'm Ann Snowden." Make a comment. Your seatmates may or may not choose to introduce themselves and engage in conversation, but you have successfully done your part.

Passing a friend at the mall while you are with another friend does not require an introduction, but if that friend stops to talk with the two of you, then you should introduce them.

■■ ■■ ■■

A View of Manners from Bible Days

In John 1:40–42 we find the story of two brothers, Andrew and Simon (Peter), who were fishermen. Andrew had heard Jesus speak and was so moved by Jesus' message that he wanted his brother Simon to meet Jesus. Andrew is mentioned only a few times in Scripture, but notice what an important thing he did. He brought his brother to meet the Lord Jesus.

Later Jesus gave Simon the name *Peter*, which means "rock." Peter became one of Jesus' greatest followers. After Peter met Jesus, his goals and priorities changed. He was changed by Jesus' love and spent his life communicating that love to others. He introduced hundreds of people to Christ.

Like Andrew, we should take seriously our responsibility to introduce people. We never know how important an introduction might be.

Dr. Mordecai Hamm introduced Billy Graham to the Lord, and we marvel at how many people he has introduced to Christ in his lifetime.

Andrew's Introduction

Andrew, Simon Peter's brother, was one of the two who heard John and followed Him [Christ]. He first found his own brother Simon and told him, "We have found the Messiah!" (which means "Anointed One"), and he brought Simon to Jesus. When Jesus saw him, He said, "You are Simon, son of John. You will be called Cephas" (which means "Rock") (John 1:40–42).

Chapter 4

Making Conversation

One of the hardest parts of meeting new people is knowing how to make pleasant conversation or small talk, sometimes called chatting. If the introducer gives you some information about the other person during the introduction, you may find that helpful as a starting point. You can ask an open-ended question, one that requires more than a yes or no answer. "Tom tells me you have just moved here. Where are you working (or living or going to school)?"

> *Silence is one great art of conversation.*—William Hazlitt

Ideal communication is an even exchange of thought, ideas, and information. Each person in the conversation has about the same amount of time to talk.

Communication is a lot more than tossing out some words in public. It's a skill you can learn. Think of it as playing a game with a ball. One person talks awhile and then listens (tosses the ball) for the other person to talk. Listening is an important part of having a conversation.

Tips for Good Communication

- Listen attentively while the other person is talking. Interruptions are always annoying. Wait for a pause when you are certain the other person has completed his thought.
- To break the ice, bring up simple and general topics such as the surroundings, the occasion that brings you together, or how you

know the mutual friend who introduced you. The weather is a last resort, but it's always on people's mind.

- Other general topics are family, school, hobbies, work, movies, books, entertainment, vacations, church, places you have lived, pets, sports, or other activities.
- Don't ask personal questions that you would not like for someone to ask you, such as "How much money do you make?"
- Other topics to stay away from when you are talking to an acquaintance you don't know well are health, age, weight, marital status, and ethnicity.
- At the dinner table avoid subjects about dieting and those that are unpleasant to the appetite or argumentative, such as politics or religious doctrine.
- Don't try to impress people with big words, but build a vocabulary that you can draw from to talk intelligently about a number of subjects.
- If more than one person is in the conversation, make sure others get a chance to express their viewpoint. You can say, "John, what do you think about it?"
- Be sincere, but find at least one kind or complimentary remark you can make to the person you are talking to, such as, "Congratulations on your promotion."
- Accept compliments graciously without making excuses. Simply say, "Thank you. You are kind to notice."
- Never finish others' sentences for them. Be patient while they think of the right words to say.
- Acknowledge important events or accomplishments in the life of the person with whom you are talking.
- Maintain eye contact by looking from the person's mouth, back to the eyes, and around the face, but never look away from the face. Perhaps you would feel more comfortable looking between the person's eyes.
- Do not interrupt or monopolize a conversation by trying to showcase your charm or wit.
- Don't ramble on about yourself, your family, or your troubles.
- If you disagree with the person you are talking to, do so pleasantly and respectfully. You may need to change the subject if it appears to be displeasing to others in the group.
- Avoid changing the subject if others seem to be pleased and interested.
- Develop a sense of humor. Never laugh when others are being put down, but laugh at yourself when it's appropriate.

- Don't be a complainer or a criticizer.
- Don't give advice unless someone asks for it.
- Never be a name-dropper. Mentioning names of prominent or important people makes you sound insecure.
- Some things are better left unsaid. Just because you know it doesn't mean you have to tell it. Avoid gossip.
- Be honest without being brutally honest. Either find one nice thing to say about something or someone, or say nothing at all.
- Don't use flattery because it is usually untrue or exaggerated praise. Flattery embarrasses people.
- Avoid using jargon or slang that others may not understand and never use foul language or profanity.
- If you are asked a question too personal to answer, turn it around with humor. For instance, if someone asks if your hair is your natural color, laugh and say, "Only my hairdresser knows for sure." If someone asks how much money you earn, laugh and say, "Not nearly enough, I assure you."

Conversation with Acquaintances and Seldom Seen Friends

Often you are expected to make conversation with friends and acquaintances you don't see often. These people's lives may have changed dramatically since you last saw them. According to Debra Fine, author of *The Fine Art of Small Talk*, you should use caution when asking specifics such as "How's your job?" or "How's your husband?" The job may have ended, and the couple may no longer be married. A safe question would be "What's been going on with work and family since the last time I talked to you?"[1]

Shallow but fun topics such as hot pop-culture matters are usually safe. They include the bowl games, the World Series baseball games, current movies, new fads, cell phones and how other people's phones drive you crazy but you can't live without yours, personal digital assistants and how helpful yours is, how DVD discs remember all that information, and other "gotta-get-em" gadgets.

When you are trying to get to know someone on a deeper level of friendship or dating, you can ask more specific questions such as, "Have you always lived here? Tell me about your family. What's your favorite sport? What kind of books do you like to read? When you were young, what did you want to be when you grew up? What family traditions do you enjoy? What was your favorite subject in school?"

Most Important Rule

The most important rule to remember when you are talking to someone is not to say anything hurtful or mean-spirited either to the person you are talking to or about someone else.

A View of Manners from Bible Days

The Bible has much to say about how to speak—what we say and how we say it. Our conversations reveal a great deal about us. Jesus said the two greatest commandments in the Bible are to love your neighbor as yourself and to love God with all your heart. These commandments should be the basis for all our conversations with others and about others.

The Consequences of Idle Words

In Matthew 12:24–37 Jesus healed the demon-possessed man who was blind and unable to speak. When the religious leaders (the Pharisees) saw and heard it, they regaled Jesus by saying, "The man drives out demons only by Beelzebub, the ruler of the demons" (v. 24).

Jesus answered them by calling them a "brood of vipers!" He went on to say, "How can you speak good things when you are evil? For the mouth speaks from the overflow of the heart. . . . I tell you that on the day of judgment people will have to account for every careless word they speak. For by your words you will be acquitted, and by your words you will be condemned" (vv. 34, 36–37).

Chapter 5

Dressing to Achieve

Whether you are going for a job interview or simply going to work everyday, the way you dress, your overall appearance, says a lot about the way you feel, work, and live. A slovenly appearance gives the impression that you are untidy and careless.

As mentioned in chapter 2, first impressions are made within the first thirty seconds of meeting someone. Appearance is a big part of that. The way we package ourselves is important. "Job applicants who project the professional image effectively even command higher starting salaries—as much as 20 percent more—than those who do not."[1] The traditional work wardrobe changed little for almost a century. It was a suit, shirt, and tie for men and dresses and suits for women. Then in the early 1990s, casual Friday was introduced. Eventually some companies and organizations adopted casual dress for every other day as well.

Now in the twenty-first century, we are seeing a modest return to the traditional way of dressing, if not a complete return, in all corporations. Executives have found that the way businesspersons dress affects the way they conduct business, and that affects the profit margin.

The man with a polished, pressed look with lace-up shoes tends to have an air of efficiency and attentiveness to detail. People tend to judge our status, character, and abilities by the way we dress.

Marilou Berry of the Scripps Howard News Service reports that Mark Weber, president of Phillips Van-Heusen Corporation, has this to say: "Because all clothing sends a message, it's important to decide early on what message you wish to convey. Some people strongly believe that the trend to business casual dressing has gone too far, and that it can mean a casualty for companies."

Fashion-trend watcher and clothing authority Tom Julian with the New York advertising agency Fallon McElligott says, "The pendulum is swinging the other way." While Julian admits people like to be casual, he says he's not surprised some offices are reversing the trend. "It's kind of like when women got out of corsets and hats. It was a relief at the time but many are back into them."

Considering the mixture of business casual and more conservative apparel in the workplace today, the job seeker should ask about the style of dress before applying for work at a particular company.

The Man's Suit

The fabric you choose for your clothing makes a difference. There are two kinds of fabric, natural and man-made fibers. One kind made of natural fibers such as linen, wool, and cotton is known for its ability to hold its shape and allow air to pass through for comfort. Natural fibers are preferable for business attire and considered more professional than the man-made ones. Polyester, acetate, and nylon are popular artificial fabrics, but popular does not always equal good taste.

The only advantage to buying clothes made of synthetic fibers is that they are washable and do not shrink or wrinkle easily. They travel well. It is possible and even recommended that you buy clothes of natural fibers with a small amount of synthetic in order to reap the benefits of both types of fabric. Another option is the new Microfiber.

The Best Fit

Since both fit and style are important, you should only go to a reputable clothier to shop. Buying your business clothes off the sale rack may be tempting, but your appearance is important enough to buy the best you can afford. When looking at the price tag, consider how many times you will be able to wear the item. Even some on-sale items don't measure up to that test. Ask yourself how many times a week or a year you can wear the item.

In upscale men's stores, alterations are usually provided at no charge. The store will have a tailor there to fit the clothes to you, perhaps are making the price of the garment worth it. You want to make sure a suit fits across the shoulders without wrinkling. A reputable store will keep only the latest style in lapel widths that change from year to year.

When you shop for a suit, take the shirt, shoes, and anything else you may wear with it in order to get a better fit and overall look. Of course, you may be purchasing new accessories as well. When you try on clothes, remember to carry in your pockets whatever you usually carry because that can affect the way something fits. (Bulging pockets are never the look of the professional.)

The same holds true for the businesswoman's suit. Silk is a strong fiber for blouses; and even though it may cost more, it will be attractive for years.

Color is an important part of your purchase. Dark blue and dark gray are good conservative colors for any business professional. Two other good choices for men are the dark blue pinstripe and the gray pinstripe. In warm climates you will need a lightweight summer suit. Unless the business is very conservative such as a financial institution, a navy blue blazer and gray slacks or skirt make a nice alternative to the suit-every-day look.

The Style

In choosing the style, you will need to consider single or double-breasted suits and jackets. The vents in the jacket will either be on the sides, in the center back, or there will be no vents at all. Double-breasted suits are not flattering to short, stout men.

When a man wears a double-breasted jacket, he keeps it buttoned at all times. For a single-breasted suit, he buttons it when he is standing and opens it when he is seated.

The Shirt

When buying a shirt for the suit, look for long-sleeved, barrel cuffs with whatever collar is in style at the time. That may be a collar clasped with a gold pin, or it may be a straight pointed collar. Button-down oxford cloth shirts are often too casual for business, depending on the type of place where you work. Save them for casual days or company outings. In a reputable men's clothing store, you can trust the salesclerk to know which collars are in current style.

A white or off-white shirt of 100 percent cotton is preferred in the business world. It should be worn crisply starched. You can buy shirts that are part cotton and part synthetic, but they will turn yellow in the laundry. The shirt collar should feel comfortable with two fingers between your neck and the collar.

When wearing the shirt with a suit, the shirt sleeve should be visible about one-half inch below the sleeve of the jacket. Monogrammed cuffs are not professional looking.

Traditionally, executives' shirts did not have pockets. Shirt pockets were designed to hold "tools"—pens, pencils, eyeglasses. For the true executive, these implements belong in other places—in the suit jacket pocket or briefcase, for example.[2]

The Tie

When buying a tie to go with your new suit, look for a silk tie. It is more versatile and more correct. Tell the salesclerk the type of business you will be doing and ask his or her help in selecting the right pattern for your tie. Financial institutions and other conservative companies prefer subtle, subdued ties with a small pattern or none at all.

The standard "four-in-hand" is the most appropriate knot for your tie. The tip of your tie should stop about the center of your belt buckle.

"Ties on short men tend to be too long. Some men solve this problem during the tying process by giving the tie one extra wrap around before making the knot. These men might also use a full-Windsor knot, which takes up more material than the basic four-in-hand or Windsor knots. Unfortunately, ties on tall or large men often dangle somewhere in the lower-belly range. In cases like that, men can buy extra-long ties."[3]

Socks

Socks are more important than you might think. White athletic socks do not belong in the business world, except perhaps before or after work when you go to your athletic club to work out. Your shoes for these after-hours activities will, of course, be of the athletic type also.

When wearing trousers, make sure your socks are long enough to cover the calf of your leg when you cross your legs. A hairy leg should never be in sight. It can destroy an otherwise stellar appearance.

Shoes

The style of shoe you choose will say a lot about you as well. The corporate man usually chooses a laced, plain-toe oxford, and a professional male may wear a tasseled loafer. Shoes should be of the best quality leather for durability and a long-lasting, comfortable fit.

Shoes should always be polished with well-kept heels and soles. Run-down heels and bottoms with holes don't make you look poor; they show that you don't take care of details. Without your realizing it, an interviewer may look at your heels and soles to check for that.

Martha Stewart says, "Shoes should be routinely cleaned with a leather soap, then polished with a wax-based polish to restore shine and cover scratches. About once a month, condition leather shoes with a liquid or cream leather conditioner to keep them supple."[4]

Belts and Buckles

For a gray, navy, or charcoal man's suit, choose a black belt. It should be about one inch wide with a brass buckle. No decorated belts of any kind are appropriate in the business world. Wear a brown belt with brown shoes and a black belt with black or cordovan shoes.

Business Casual for Men

If casual days are practiced where you work, the following should be the minimum requirements:

- No shorts, jeans, or sneakers.
- No clothing with holes, tears, or fringe.
- Shirts with a collar, even on a recreational shirt.
- Shirts free of logos (except your company logo), slogans, or artwork.
- Only company caps or head gear.
- Button-up shirts with a collar, but no tie is a good choice for casual days.

Improper dress is the most common reason job candidates are eliminated.[5]

—John Molloy, *The New Women's Dress for Success*

The Businesswoman's Attire

Before the 1970s, men dominated the business world. Then when the "women's movement" came along, more and more women went to work. In the early years women tried to copy the look of their male counterparts. They wore suits with skirts made of the same fabric men bought, and their blouses often had pointed or button-down collars. Some women even wore ties.

Today women can have equal status, position, and salary without denying their femininity. They can be conservative without being drab. They dress for credibility. It's always a good idea for a woman to watch to see what the most highly ranked women wear in the company where she works or where she wants to work.

The Woman's Suit

You can never go wrong if you choose a classic, single-breasted suit or coatdress. The best colors are gray, navy, and black. When you go shopping, look for wide seams and clothes that are fully lined. The lining will make for a better fit, and the outfit will look new longer.

If you prefer dresses, look for a long-sleeved coatdress with a single or double row of buttons or a dress with a jacket. Short-sleeved coatdresses are acceptable. Pantsuits for women are acceptable in some businesses. It's better to wear a suit with a skirt to a job interview.

The Fabric and Color

Go to upscale stores that sell women's clothes so that you can feel the quality of the fabric and check the seams for width and edging to prevent raveling. The hem should be at least one and a half inches deep. Even if you can't afford to buy the best, you will know what to look for. As with men's clothing, natural fibers or a mixture of natural and synthetic make the best choice for the woman's business wardrobe. Garments made of all polyester stand out conspicuously.

The best colors are dark or subdued with little or no pattern. Black, gray, and navy are good choices. If you prefer bright colors, remember that loud colors attract attention. People will remember and count the times you wear a red dress. You don't want to be remembered for your attire but for your expertise.

A Good Fit

The best fit is one that is not too tight or too revealing and does not bulge. When you try on a suit, wear the blouse you plan to wear with it to check for a comfortable fit. Go to a reputable women's shop that specializes in clothes for the working world.

Accessories

A woman can keep her individuality by choosing the right accessories. A caveat: less is better. You can wear so many accessories they detract from your businesslike image. A string of classic pearls or a gold or silver chain can add a touch of distinction to your outfit without overpowering your look.

Earrings should be chosen with care. Hoop earrings or ones that dangle are never appropriate. Pearl earrings are a good choice as well as small gold or silver ones. Only one earring in each ear is appropriate. Nice silk scarves can change your outfit from one day to the next. Rings are better left at home, except for wedding and engagement rings. Bracelets can be a real annoyance when they clank together on the desk.

Purses and Briefcases

If you carry a briefcase and a handbag, buy the best leather you can afford and be prepared to put your small purse in your briefcase or hang your purse from your shoulder so that you will have your right hand free to shake hands at all times. If you go to lunch or dinner and leave your briefcase behind, your purse should be small enough to rest on your lap while you eat.

Shoes

When you buy shoes, look for closed-toe, medium-heel pumps in a dark color such as navy, burgundy, or black. In summer you may wear beige or taupe. Shoes in pastel colors don't look businesslike.

Hosiery

Your hosiery should be so plain and inconspicuous that it is virtually unnoticeable. Wearing colored or patterned hosiery to work is a no-no, no matter how well it matches your skirt. Wearing no hosiery to work may be comfortable and somewhat "in style" today, but a businesswoman always looks better in hosiery, no matter the temperature.

Nontraditional Workplace

If you are entering or applying for a job in a nontraditional office setting, dress the way the best-dressed person that works there dresses.

If you are dressed for an interview or going to work on your job, you may incorrectly assume that if no one says anything negative about your appearance, you are appropriately dressed. The truth is that if the boss or a coworker calls attention to your appearance, it has probably been bothersome for some time. The damage to your image may have already been done.

Men's Dressy Casual for Going Out

Men should always wear a shirt with a collar. If the invitation says "casual," find out where and what the activities will be to help you decide the proper attire. If you are not sure what is expected, you may choose the safest way to dress, which is a button-up shirt and a sport coat, such as a navy blue blazer, and khakis or slacks. No tie. Never wear a sport coat with suit trousers. You can always take the jacket off if other men there are not wearing one. Dressy casual usually means a jacket, but you can always take it off.

Another option, if you leave work for an early after-work party or get-together, wear your suit but remove your tie. That way everyone knows you do not want to overdress but that you have simply come from work.

The shirt can be a small plaid or a solid color. Leather shoes such as loafers and a belt complete the outfit.

A more casual option is a polo shirt with a collar and slacks. You can even add a casual sport coat to that outfit, if you like. Loafers would be appropriate.

If you get an invitation to a formal dinner in someone's home, wear a suit and tie.

Business Casual for Women

The key to dressing professionally even on casual days is to remember that it is not Saturday casual. Many women shop in the women's department of a conservative men's store. Your casual clothes should cost about the same and be of the same quality as your other business clothes.

On June 20, 1897, the Arkansas Democrat-Gazette *published this news: "With the month of June come all the summer pleasures, and it behooveth the careful woman to get her bathing suit in order. A skirt reaching just below the knees is deemed most modest and inconspicuous. The skirts are made quite full."*

Bad choices for women on casual days are jeans, shorts, culottes, and stretch pants. If you work in a labor-intensive job, jeans or khakis may be appropriate. Watch to see if your superiors wear them.

To test your professional image, look in the mirror before you leave for an interview or for work and ask yourself if you are dressed appropriately—not too faddish, not too comfortable, and not too carefree. John Molloy says, "Don't let your clothing get in the way of business."

Women's Dressy Casual for Going Out

Slacks with or without a jacket are appropriate, as well as a nice, casual skirt and blouse. For a formal dinner in someone's home, a dressy dress is appropriate.

Formal Wear for Men

When an invitation arrives with the words *white tie* or *black tie*, what does it mean?

White Tie

The most formal dress is white tie. It is never worn before 6:00 P.M. White tie calls for a black tailcoat or frock coat with matching pants, white shirt with stiff wing collar, starched white waistcoat (vest) and white bow tie. A crisp white handkerchief shows from the topcoat pocket. Optional accessories include: silk top hat, white silk scarf, and white gloves.

Black Tie

Black tie attire is also not worn before 6:00 P.M., except for late-afternoon weddings. It calls for a traditional black dinner jacket (tuxedo) with, if single-breasted, a cummerbund or vest (never both), white shirt, and bow tie (preferably black). In warm weather, a lightweight white jacket can sub for the black jacket. The pants are black with a satin stripe down the side. Optional accessories: black homburg (hat), white silk scarf, and gray suede gloves.

Black Tie Optional

When the invitation says black-tie optional, men may wear a dark business suit with a white shirt and a tie, usually in a solid color such as silver.

Formal Wear for Women

When the invitation says *white tie*, the lady wears a floor-length, formal-type dress. For black-tie occasions she wears either a cocktail-length (mid-calf) or a floor-length dress, depending on the custom in the area. For black-tie optional, she may wear a cocktail dress or a knee-length black dress.

:: :: ::

A View of Manners from Bible Days

"The manner of dress today in the Eastern countries is much the same as it was centuries ago." "Thus, the prevailing Palestinian dress of modern times (except for the Jews who have gone back to Israel from various parts of the world) is much as it was in the epoch that produced the Bible."

The men wear an inner garment (tunic or shirt), a girdle (to serve as a belt), an outer garment, or mantle, a headdress, and sandals. The outer garment or mantle serves as an overcoat. "It was the outer garment or mantle with which Elijah smote the waters of Jordan and crossed over with Elisha, and when he was taken up into heaven this mantle became the property of Elisha."[6]

Jesus' Robe

When the soldiers crucified Jesus, they took His clothes and divided them into four parts, a part for each soldier. They also took the tunic [mantle], which was seamless, woven in one piece from the top. So they said to one another, "Let's not tear it, but toss for it, to see who gets it."

They did this to fulfill the Scripture that says: "They divided My clothes among themselves, and for My clothing they cast lots" (John 19:23–24).

"The garment of Jesus for which the Roman soldiers cast lots, was a *tunic* without seam. It has often been referred to as a robe, but this is not correct, for it was not his outer garments, but rather his *undergarment*. Unfortunate translations have been responsible for this erroneous idea."[7]

Women's Attire

Women's dress differed in detail rather than in kind. They also wore a tunic, a cloak, and a veil that was the distinctive piece of female apparel. They also wore more ornamentation such as rings, bracelets, and earrings.

In 1 Peter 3:3–4, Peter has this to say to the women, "Your beauty should not be the outer beauty of elaborate hairstyles and the wearing of gold ornaments or of fine clothes; rather, it should be an inner beauty with the imperishability of a gentle and quiet spirit, which is very valuable in God's eyes."

Earrings were at one time worn by the women of Jacob's family (Genesis 35:4 NASB). And the golden earrings of the Israelite women contributed to the making by Aaron of the golden calf (Exodus 32:2 NASB)."[8]

Chapter 6

Manners in Public Places

> *The greater man the greater courtesy.*—Alfred, Lord Tennyson

In public places your manners are on display. Public embarrassment can be painful, but if you remember the Golden Rule, you will act toward others the way you would like them to act toward you. You will be courteous and thoughtful. Usually, but not in all incidents, you will be treated by others the way you treat them. If you are loud and obnoxious, others will likely avoid your company.

Be socially aware of your surroundings. That is, always remember that you are not alone and that your behavior is always under scrutiny in public. We think little of children chattering in quiet places with no embarrassment. But when adults behave disruptively or conspicuously, we are embarrassed for them or angry with them.

To conduct yourself in an adult manner, keep your voice down and your conversations private. Greet acquaintances with a smile. If you want to stop and talk, don't stop in the middle of a walkway but go with your friend to a place where you will not be in the way.

Anything that attracts attention should be avoided. Consideration for others rules out whistling, singing, laughing boisterously, calling out another person's name, and shouting while in public, whether you are alone or with friends.

Your behavior in public should be marked by quiet dignity. Socially, males still defer to females, and everyone should defer to the elderly. In business, deference is based on seniority; however, even in business, a man should always be a gentleman, and a woman should behave in a ladylike fashion. Certain social situations need specific attention, including walking on the sidewalk, entering doorways and elevators, and being in other public places.

In public parks, pools, health clubs, shopping malls, golf and tennis facilities, beaches, and playgrounds, always clean up after yourself, discarding tissues, gum wrappers, popcorn containers, soda cans, unwanted program inserts, or whatever debris you have created in the proper receptacle. At athletic facilities pick up your sweaty towels and place them in the proper place and return equipment in good shape. The more mature people are, the more responsibility they take for their own actions.

General Guidelines for Entertainments

Emily Post gives us some general courtesies that are simply "basic, civilized behavior at any entertainment":

- Plan to arrive on time.
- No talking during any part of any performance.
- Hats off, hair trimmed, heads upright. It is most discouraging to have paid a large sum of money to view a performance and to find oneself unable to view anything but the backs of big-haired or hatted people or a couple with their heads pressed together.
- Feet on the floor, not on the seats around you or on your own seat.
- No throwing of any item into the audience or at the performers on stage.
- No booing, hissing, or rude noises. If you do not like a performance of course refrain from clapping, but to express your displeasure volubly is rude. Do not express approval or disapproval with gasps, groans, sighs, or comments.
- Do respect smoke-free environments, even those of outdoor amphitheaters. Not only is it a courtesy, but it also may be the law.
- Remove crying, screaming, chattering, or otherwise noisy children immediately.
- If your cough becomes a prolonged noisy bout, remove yourself. After you have stopped coughing, return to your seat when it is not disruptive to others to do so.
- Do not spit chewing gum on the floor or stick it under seats. Wrap it in paper and dispose of it in a waste receptacle.
- Always rise for the national anthem; also rise for an anthem of another country.
- Always rise for the Pledge of Allegiance to the Flag. Rise, as well, for a pledge to another country's flag, a courtesy that does not include pledging allegiance to that country.

- Do not hum, sing along, or keep time with fingers or feet unless invited to do so by the performers. Others in the audience should not have to listen to your rendition of what is being performed on stage.
- If you wear a beeper, you should have it immediately accessible so that you can turn it off instantly if you are being paged. It's better to have a vibrating beeper.
- If you have a cell phone, you should say excuse me and answer it quickly when it rings or turn it off.[1]

On the Street

There is a valued reason for every rule of etiquette; however, some of the rules are based only on tradition and custom because the reason no longer exists. For instance, it used to be that a man walked on the curbside of the sidewalk when walking with a lady to protect her from splashes of mud thrown up by carriage or wagon wheels. Paved roads have eliminated the need for such protection, but men should continue to walk on the street side, unless he needs to protect a woman from muggers and purse snatchers lurking in doorways. Using common sense, he would then walk on the inside, always choosing the most protective side.

To escort a woman for any reason, a man extends his bent arm for her to take hold of it with her hand. If she is holding onto him, she will not likely fall as she might if he takes her elbow.

Public display of affection, often called PDA, is never appropriate beyond the greeting of a quick kiss on the cheek or a hug from the side.

Push and Pull Doors

Men open pull doors and hold them for women to pass through. For heavy push doors, men should go through first and hold them open for anyone coming behind them. No one should let a door fly back in someone's face.

Anyone who has a door opened for him or her should always say thank you.

Revolving Doors

Women can enter revolving doors first if the door is positioned for easy entrance. The man gets in and pushes from behind. However, if the door is not easy to enter, the man steps into a compartment first and turns the door slightly for the woman to enter behind him.

Elevators, Escalators, and Stairs

Men should let women enter and leave an uncrowded elevator first. When it is crowded, the people nearest the door get off first. You should turn to hold the doors open for others to exit. The person closest to the "door open" button may hold it and remain on the elevator for everyone who wishes to exit.

The people exiting an elevator should be given the opportunity to leave before you try to enter. Then, to facilitate traffic, you should step to the rear or as far back on one side as possible. Give the number of your floor and say "Please." If you make any comments, keep your voice low. You must make room for those who want to leave before you do, so step out to let them exit if you are in the front of a crowded elevator. If the situation is reversed, say, "Excuse me" to anyone who may be blocking your exit.

If the elevator is not crowded, a man should remove his hat or cap. If you are carrying an umbrella, hold the pointed end down so that you do not poke someone.

If you are standing near the control panel of the elevator, be prepared to punch in the floor numbers as they are called and push the "open door" button to hold the doors open as others exit.

A man goes down escalators and stairs first but goes up escalators and stairs last in order to protect the woman from a fall. When exiting an escalator, move quickly out of the way. It is dangerous to block the exit while trying to decide which way to go.

Restaurant Doors

What to do? The male may find that when he opens the door for his date or spouse that a crowd of people march through leaving him in an awkward "holding" pattern. To extricate himself he should move away from the door until he can barely reach it, hoping someone with the crowd of people will take his place.

Sometimes a restaurant door has another door with a small area between it and the door that opens into the main restaurant. A man should open the outer door for his companion, who waits in the anteroom for him to open the second door. If someone else opens the second door, the individual waits in the main lobby of the restaurant. If the anteroom becomes crowded, the individual should open the second door and wait inside.

Wearing Hats in Public

A man should remove his hat or cap when he enters almost any building such as a restaurant, a church, a private home, a movie, or theater lobby. He should remove it when the American flag goes by and while the national anthem or his school song, or that of a rival school, is being played or sung. Wearing caps or hats in restaurants seems to be the biggest complaint among patrons. You may feel free to wear them in gymnasiums.

If a man enters a crowded elevator, he may keep his hat on to prevent crushing it or being in someone's way. He may keep it on his head while watching a sporting event in a gymnasium.

On Public Transportation

Pushing and shoving on trains, buses, and subways is rude; but a well-mannered person tries to ignore the rudeness of others and be as considerate of fellow passengers as he or she would like them to be. Some things to avoid are poking or tripping people with an umbrella or briefcase, stepping on others' feet, taking up more space with your packages than is needed, or unnecessarily blocking the aisle. It is not in good taste to talk loudly to someone you might recognize. The thoughtful person does not read a newspaper over someone's shoulder or open windows before asking permission of those around him.

Talking or laughing loudly with your friends may seem harmless and reasonable to you, but in reality you are invading the space of the people around you and being annoying. Remember that noise is amplified in enclosed spaces.

A woman should precede a man when they enter a bus, train, plane, or subway together. The man should exit first in order to help her. In a movie theater he leads the way and chooses the row if there is no usher. Then she enters the row and sits first.

A woman should offer her seat to anyone who may need it more than she does. A man offers his seat to a woman, someone with a disability, and the elderly. If the woman is offered a seat and she takes it, she should say thank you.

Taxis

It is usually against the law for anyone to get out or in a taxi on the traffic side. It is safer for the man to enter a taxi first. (The driver could drive off.) Then the woman enters, not having to slide across the seat. He then reaches across her to close the door. If the man is seated on the side next to the curb with a woman beside him, he should jump out and help her get out on his side. If she is on the curbside, he should reach over and unlatch the door so that she can exit first. If there is no traffic problem, he can get out and walk around the car to help her out. (For tipping information, see appendix C.)

Shopping Sense

When you go shopping, you must wait your turn for service; besides, the people ahead of you are probably in a hurry too. Maneuvering yourself ahead of others, flagging down salesclerks, or interrupting them when they are busy with someone else marks you as being selfish. You should grant salesclerks the same courtesy that you give other people.

Be careful not to block aisles with your body, bags, or cart, and do not delay clerks by engaging friends in long conversations.

Church Manners

Always enter a church quietly and reverently in time for the beginning of the service. Men remove their hats. If you are late, wait in the foyer for a break in the service when an usher may seat you. The woman follows the usher and the man follows her. But if there is no usher, the man leads the way down the aisle, finds the row, and steps aside for the woman to enter the row and be seated first. If the seats are in the middle of the row, he leads the way in front of the people seated, and she follows him.

No one should whisper, giggle, chew gum, read anything not a part of the service, write notes, stare at people, or turn around and look behind for any reason, except when a bride is coming down the aisle. You may nod and smile at friends, but you should not call out greetings.

If you are visiting a church not your own, be respectful and observant, careful to follow the ritual as much as you can. You may join in the worship, but you should take communion only if you are invited to do so. When you are visiting a church where you are unfamiliar with the ritual, it is not necessary for you to participate in the service. It is necessary, however, that you be respectful of others' beliefs, sacraments, ordinances, and customs. You are like a visitor in someone's home.

Manners in the Car

If you are a passenger in a car, you should ask permission before opening or closing windows or adjusting the heat, the air conditioning, or the radio. The driver should be attentive to the needs of the passengers.

If you are driving a car, park carefully. Avoid taking up two parking spaces. When you parallel park, make sure the cars in front of and behind you can get out easily.

If another driver is rude, don't show your anger or make any gestures. If you do, the other driver's manners will not improve, and you may be putting yourself in danger if he chooses to retaliate.

Theaters, Museums, and Performance Halls

Arrive early. You should be seated before the ceremony or performance begins. If you must be late, wait for the intermission (or proper interlude) to find your seat. It's polite to apologize as you pass by those who are already seated.

If you must seat yourself because the ushers are busy and you find someone sitting in what appears to be your seats, check the tickets and quietly say, "I believe you are sitting in our seats." If this polite remark does not prompt the intruder to move, you should find an usher to take care of the problem, giving him or her your tickets. Your companions should wait at the back of the theater until you have secured the correct seats. They should not tag along behind you all over the theater.

Don't carry large purses, bags, or other paraphernalia not absolutely necessary. If you must carry something, don't swing your possessions and bump others as you pass.

Silence is mandatory. It is distracting to be seated near someone who is rattling a program, asking questions, or commenting on what is happening on stage or screen.

If you have to leave your seat to go to the concession area or to the rest room, simply say "Excuse me" and wait for the others on the row to let you pass. It is polite for those seated to stand while you slip past them, being careful not to step on toes.

If you enter a row of seats with your back to the stage, you can see other's feet to avoid as you make your way down the row. Facing a captive audience also keeps one's derriere out of the other's faces. If you prefer to face the stage, step gingerly without bending at the waist.

When the program is completed, applaud appropriately, and leave with the flow of patrons in your section. Don't climb over the people in front of you as you try to rush out of the building.

Applause

Clap with the fingers of one hand in the other palm. Clapping palm on palm sounds like slapping. Don't clap your hands in front of your face. Shoulder level is better. Don't clap after others have ceased, no matter how enthusiastic your response.

Applauding at the wrong time can be rude and embarrassing. For instance, at the opera you may applaud at the end of an aria and after each curtain, but not for the entrances or exits of a performer. Applaud when the conductor first walks out at the beginning and after intermissions.

Ballet

When at the ballet, wait to applaud until a complete dance or scene is over. Individual performances are applauded at the end of the ballet, never during. Applaud the conductor the same way you do for the opera.

The Symphony

You should always applaud the conductor and guest soloists when they walk out on stage. But clapping stops when the conductor steps onto the platform and raises the baton. Applause for the music is held until the conductor turns around toward the audience and bows.

At the Movies

When going to a movie, you may hold a place in line while your companion parks the car, but you should not hold places in line for a van or busload of people planning to join you.

When you are inside the theater and reach your row, a man lets the woman go in first unless there are people with them. Then one of the men enters the row first with the two women, and the other man follows behind. That way, the women are seated in the middle. If the seats are in the middle of the row, the man leads the way in front of all the people, and she follows him to the open seats.

Once the movie begins, don't talk, move constantly, kick the back of the chair, or put your feet on the chair in front of you. Don't trek back and forth to the snack bar or make noise with your refreshments such as slurping, chomping, crumpling candy wrappers, popping gum, or shaking boxes. Don't stretch your arms and block the view for rows behind you.

If you must sneeze or cough, muffle it if you can. If an episode of either one overtakes you, quietly slip out, excusing yourself as you pass.

Don't express displeasure with groans, sighs, gasps, head movements, or loud laughter. In other words, be as still and quiet as you would like the other patrons to be.

Polite Manners with Rude People

Remember that some people have never had the opportunity to learn simple social skills. Though we think the rules should be common sense, we must realize that some offenders do not mean to misbehave. Often they will change their conduct when they are gently reminded that they are disturbing others.

"'Whenever you feel like criticizing any one,' he told me, 'just remember that all the people in this world haven't had the advantages that you've had.'"

—F. Scott Fitzgerald, *The Great Gatsby*

If someone nearby disturbs you, say, "I am sorry, but I can't hear the performance [movie or speaker]." If the noise continues, you may ask an usher to call the manager. The alternative is to move to another available seat.

One etiquette authority says staring "more in pity than in anger" at the perpetrator is often the most effective way to deal with rude people.

Manners with the Disabled

The proper term for someone with a disability is "individual with a disability." Think of the individual first and then the disability. Instead of referring to someone as a deaf man, say a man with a hearing impairment. Someone dying of cancer is a person living with cancer.

> *The word* handicapped *goes back in English history to when the British crown gave licenses and special caps to disabled veterans of war so they could beg on the street for a living.*

Most individuals with a disability prefer we not think of their handicap first. They want the same independence and acceptance as able-bodied persons. Therefore, avoid terms that suggest negative feelings of dependency, pity, and disease.

To avoid embarrassing yourself or the individual with a disability, there are a few important rules to observe.

- Never point or stare at someone who looks different in any way.
- Before grabbing a wheelchair or someone's arm, ask politely if you can be of help. People with disabilities pride themselves on being as independent as possible, but sometimes your help is welcome. The key is to ask and not to be condescending or pitying in your manner or tone of voice. Give the individual the opportunity to accept or decline your offer to help.
- If your offer is accepted, ask how you may help. This indicates that you recognize the person is not totally dependent.
- Avoid appearing to be impatient with the person if he or she declines your offer of assistance and then takes twice as long to accomplish a task.

Shaking Hands with the Disabled

When you are introduced to persons with an infirmed right hand or an artificial hand, let them take the lead in how you greet each other. They may simply smile and say hello without offering a hand. Or they may offer an artificial right hand or offer their left hand.

If someone offers you his or her left hand, take it with your right hand. It is less awkward than using your left hand. Without realizing it, you may offer your right hand to someone with a missing hand or an artificial one. The individual will usually extend his or her left or artificial hand to make contact. Take the hand the best way you can, saying nothing about the disability and showing no surprise.

If you are a female and offer your hand first, before you know the condition of the other person's hand and that individual does not respond, say nothing. Simply withdraw your hand and continue conversing.

Above all, remember that people who are impaired will vary in their attitude about their disability. Few of us are not impaired to some degree. Our disability simply may not be as easy to see.

Public Property

Some people mistakenly think "public use" means open for public abuse. But public property deserves the same respect as your own private property. Public property is for everyone's use. Abuse is costly and nonsensical.

Never willfully damage anything or take anything that does not belong to you. Taking ashtrays and towels from restaurants and hotels is stealing, and stealing is a crime.

▇▇ ▇▇ ▇▇

A View of Manners from Bible Days

There was a generally accepted custom among the Jews to hold festivals for special events. Such occasions involved hundreds of people coming together in a public place. Some of the social times included the dedication of a newly built house, the weaning of a child, harvest time, and sheepshearing.

A New Home

According to the Mosaic law, a newly constructed dwelling was always dedicated: "Who is the man that has built a new house and has not dedicated it?" (Deut. 20:5 NASB). No doubt the social as well as the devotional element entered into the festivities.

"It was common when any person had finished a house and entered into it, to celebrate it with great rejoicing, and keep a festival, to which his friends are invited, and to perform some religious ceremonies, to secure the protection of Heaven."[2]

Chapter 7

Dating Manners

As long as there are males and females, dating will never go out of style. But the terminology used may differ from one generation to another. What used to be called "going steady" is now called "dating." Before "going steady," there were words like *promised, courting, spooning, wooing,* and other archaic descriptions. It seems that each new set of young people likes to come up with its own descriptive phrase. The *World Book Encyclopedia Dictionary* says a date is "a person of the opposite sex with whom a social appointment is made." The dictionary also gives this example for courting: "A young man courted the woman by bringing her flowers every day."

The term you use is important because it can mean keeping company with several people or spending your social time primarily with one individual. Today if you are unmarried, you are probably either "dating," meaning you date one person only, or you are "going out," which means you may go out with one person a lot but you also see other people.

Dating and going out are a lot more complicated these days. There are more questions to be answered, such as who does the asking—the man or the woman—and who pays the expenses? In the early days of the women's movement, a woman found that splitting the dinner check (also called "going Dutch") or paying for the entire evening was considered liberating to her. Dutch treat means each individual pays his or her own expenses.

Most women no longer worry about asserting their liberation and equality, at least in the dating world. Today they look for equal pay, equal status, and equal responsibility in the workplace. Even when the woman is making as much or more money than the man, he pays the tab if he asks her for the date. She can find other ways to contribute her part to the financial relationship. She can cook dinner for him or occasionally pick up theater or movie tickets. If she buys the tickets for an event, she should pick them up ahead of time and give them to him before they reach the theater, so he can present the tickets to the ticket taker.

Maureen Dowd, columnist with the *New York Times* says, "Women say they want old-fashioned courting," and a thirty-one-year-old journalist in Los Angeles says, "There is no way a woman nowadays thinks that if the man pays he is entitled to anything sexually."[1]

How a Man Asks for a Date

Ask early. Two to four days is enough time for an ordinary date, but for special occasions such as a banquet, ask about two weeks or more in advance. Exception: If a group of your friends is getting together to go for pizza and you think a new friend might like to be invited at the last minute, by all means, call her. These are usually Dutch treat dates.

You may ask in person or by telephone. Don't ask by sending someone else to ask for you, and don't E-mail your request unless you have a long-distance relationship. Never say, "What are you doing next weekend?" Say, "Would you like to go to the singles group party at church with me next Sunday evening? John and Sarah will be riding with us."

If she accepts, give her the specifics such as when you will pick her up, how you will be going, and the customary clothes if she's never been to a similar event. For a dance or other special occasion, ask two to three weeks ahead. She will need time to select the right dress and accessories. For proms, it is best to ask a month in advance.

By Telephone

When you call a woman for a date, identify yourself to whoever answers the phone. If you know her parents or roommate, say hello to them; if you don't, simply identify yourself and ask to speak to her. Never say, "Guess who this is" on the telephone. It's friendlier to chat a few minutes before asking for the date, but it's rude to ask, "What are you doing?"

You might begin with, "How did you manage getting home today in all this rain (or traffic)?" If you met at a party or church, you can talk about that briefly, but don't keep her hanging too long. Go ahead and ask if she would like to go to the game Friday night. Never say, "What are you doing Friday night?" and never be vague and too general by saying, "Would you like to go out Friday?" Be as specific as you can before expecting her answer. If she says yes, give her any other necessary information such as time, place, how you will get there, about how long you expect to be out, if and with whom you will be double-dating, and the type clothes to wear if that is not obvious. There is no need to prolong the conversation talking about other matters that you can discuss on the date. The caller always ends the conversation. End with, "If I don't see you in the meantime, I'll see you Friday night."

If she can't give you her answer immediately, ask when you might call back. If she says she already has plans, don't ask what they are. Never ask why she can't go or hint at possible reasons. Accept her answer. If she turns you down after the second attempt to make a date with her and you get the idea that she really is interested, ask her a third time, but after that, assume the answer will always be no. Bow out gracefully and save yourself some embarrassment.

> *A young adult friend of mine named Kate says she knows it's a date if he asks, he drives, and he pays.*

When a Woman Accepts or Refuses a Date

When a man asks a woman for a date, he is entitled to a prompt answer. It is rude to make him wait days for an answer. If the woman is still living at home, she may need to ask her parents, in which case she asks him if she can tell him her answer tomorrow.

The woman should remember that it often takes courage for a man to ask for a date. She should show enthusiasm and be considerate of his feelings even if he is not her first choice. It's always better to be truthful. If she says that she has to study or work that night and then he sees her out with girlfriends, he will know she lied to him. If she is not interested in him, she can do one of three things: (1) either go out with him anyway, if he has good character, (2) say she has already made plans, or (3) say, "Thank you for asking (or I appreciate your asking), but I'd rather not." A date lasts only a few hours, and she might have fun.

If she must refuse but still wants to go out with him, she can say, "I'm sorry, but I have made plans. Please ask me another time." If the man becomes a nuisance, she should say, "I'm sorry, but I would just like to be your friend."

The Arrival of the Big Night

The woman should answer the door if possible. Whoever goes to the door should invite the visitor in. He practices the six Ss and introduces himself if he does not know the parents or the roommate. The woman should be prepared to introduce her date to her parents or whoever is present. He remains standing until he is asked to sit down. If everyone sits and no one tells him to do so, he finds the nearest chair and sits erect on the front of it. He rises again if a woman enters the room for the first time.

Upon departing, the man helps the woman with her coat before putting his on and tells the people he met that it was nice to meet them. If this isn't the first meeting, he tells them it was nice to see them again. After walking to the car, he opens the car door on the passenger side while the woman gets in; then he closes the door and walks around to the driver's side. If someone else is driving, the man helps his date into the backseat.

When arriving at the destination, the man gets out, walks around, and opens the door for his date to get out. If she reaches quickly for the door handle, he can say, "Oh, let me get that for you." Opening car doors for women is just as proper today as it was long ago. Ladies always appreciate it. They should say thank you every time someone opens a door for them.

If the man gets out and walks toward the restaurant, the woman can wait for him to realize his error or simply open the door for herself. Of course, when that happens, he does not make a very good impression on her.

One Woman's Ideal Date

A young woman named Karen told me recently her idea of the perfect date. This is her account:

My ideal date calls me about a week in advance. He always has the evening planned. He tells me where we are going and with whom. If the plans change, he lets me know as soon as possible. For this ideal date I plan well what I will wear and what I might need to be a good partner on our date (tennis racquet or parka for snow sledding).

When he arrives, I greet him at the door, because if he honked, I wouldn't answer. I invite him into the house to meet my roommate (or parents), and we chat for a brief time. After arriving for the event we had planned, he opens doors for me; and he treats me with respect, introducing me to anyone I don't know.

He is neat and courteous and has a good sense of humor without being silly. He comments on what I say and makes me feel comfortable. When the evening is over, he walks me to the door where we say goodnight.

While on the date, both individuals should be attentive (not clingy) to the other. In other words, the man should be there for his date. He should focus on her and show her a good time. He should not wander off to visit with his buddies. The same goes for the woman. If either of them gets into a conversation with another friend or group of friends, it's permissible for the "left out" one to chat briefly with other friends. The key word here is *briefly*.

Saying Goodnight

At the end of a pleasant evening, all the woman owes the man is a few words about what a good time she had or how nice the evening was. Even if she did not have a good time, she can always think of something nice to say. After all, he picked her out for the date.

He, of course, walks her to the door. No gentleman simply stops the car and expects his date to get out and go to the door alone. A goodnight kiss is not mandatory and should not be expected on the first date. That time-honored tradition continues today. After a few words about how nice the evening was, simply say good-night. The man should not say "I'll call you" unless he definitely plans to do so.

If the evening is early and the woman does not live alone, she may invite him in for a while. If she lives alone, before she extends an invitation, she should be sure she knows his character and reputation well enough to be alone with him in her living room. The same could be said when reversing the genders.

A woman prefers a man with a natural, easy courtesy to the one who stiffly acts out the rules. She doesn't expect the man to be Sir Walter Raleigh and throw down his coat over the mud puddle for her to walk across. All she asks is that he respects her and does the correct thing without fanfare and without calling attention to what he is doing.

The Stay-at-Home Date

When the couple decides to spend their date time at the woman's house for the evening, she is the hostess, and he is the guest. Some points for him to remember are:

- Don't take liberties with anything.
- Don't take it literally when she says, "Make yourself at home."
- Respect the furniture. Use coasters and keep your feet off tables and food off the rug.
- Keep entertainment devices at a reasonable volume.
- Don't go into the kitchen with her unless invited.
- Offer to straighten up the room before you leave, but don't insist.

- It's all right to show interest in paintings on the wall or the father's golf trophies, but don't pick up things or snoop among the mail or other family possessions. The run of the house is not a privilege given to guests.

When the Woman Asks for the Date

In today's social environment more women are asking men out. Occasionally a woman is expected to ask a man to a party, her high school prom, her college club's dance, or the office Christmas party. Many women cringe at the idea, but if the woman is expected to bring a date, she should follow some of the same rules. She can telephone the man or ask him in person.

When she asks the man for a date, she should do so by saying, "I'd like you to be my guest for the Christmas party," or the concert, for instance. That way, he knows she is paying.

The woman's responsibility is to pay all the expenses for the event, and she should arrange for the transportation if he does not offer to do so. If the couple goes to a restaurant, the woman should suggest menu items or invite her guest to order what he likes. Beyond that, he follows the rules for being a gentleman, and she conducts herself as a lady. For instance, he should still open doors for her and assist her with her chair in the restaurant, according to etiquette expert, Dorothea Johnson of The Protocol School in Washington.®[2]

When the Man Responds to a Woman's Invitation

If a woman asks you to be her escort, try to put her at ease. Either accept graciously or decline the invitation politely and tactfully. Always thank her for inviting you even if you turn her down. If you accept, find out everything you need to know—day, time, and what to wear. Even when the woman extends the invitation, you should offer to provide the transportation. In some cases the woman may prefer to drive her car or even have the man drive her car. Such arrangements should be made when the date is made.

If a man cannot go, he should explain his reason. For example, if he likes her: "Thanks for inviting me, but I promised my brother I would take him roller blading for his birthday. I wish I could go, but maybe we can get together some other time."

If he has already accepted the invitation of another woman, just say, "Thanks for asking me, but someone else invited me a few days ago. I'll see you there."

If being in the woman's presence is more than he can bear, he should be kind when he turns her down. The man should put himself in her place and imagine how he would feel when rejected. He should feel honored to have been asked. When making an excuse, he should not be abrupt or sound annoyed. He should simply say, "I'm sorry, but I'm afraid I can't make it that night." He should not make a rash promise to call her later as an easy way out, unless he means it.

Whether you are the woman or the man, being rejected can hurt. Try not to take the rebuff too personally. It may be that the one rejecting your invitation is in love with someone else. So make a graceful exit and hope for better luck next time. When your paths cross, smile, speak, and go your way.

The Gift of Flowers from a Man

Customs vary among events and communities about giving corsages, so ask around before deciding to do so. If it is appropriate in your area to give flowers, you can select and take them yourself or have them delivered by the florist. The florist can be a big help when picking out the right flower and style of corsage. He or she will know what is popular for that particular event.

Place your order early. Ask the florist what flowers are available and ask the price. Ask a close friend of your date to find out if she wants a shoulder or wrist corsage. Find out the color of the dress she is wearing, if possible. Orchids complement any color dress. If you plan to take the corsage with you when you pick up your date, be sure to keep it in your refrigerator to keep it fresh until the big evening. When you arrive, hand the flowers to your date. Men do not pin corsages on their dates. The woman, parent, or a roommate will do that.

When corsages are appropriate, it is customary for the woman to give her date a boutonniere (a small flower, usually a carnation) for his lapel.

Dating Do's and Don'ts for Both Men and Women

- Be a good sport and have a good sense of humor. Tell only clean jokes. Don't tell or laugh at off-color or ethnic jokes.
- Show a sincere interest and pride in the achievements of your date.
- Know something about world affairs or what's going on in your area so you can make intelligent conversation.
- Choose entertainment that you both will like.
- If your date chooses a wholesome activity but one that you have never done before, be willing to try something new. Don't be a party pooper.
- Say thank you when you are paid a compliment. Don't giggle.

- Be polite to his or her friends.
- Girls should be ladies, and guys should be gentlemen.
- Be a good listener.
- Don't be possessive.
- Don't be too eager and aggressive.
- Don't call too often and become a pest.
- Don't talk about former girlfriends/boyfriends.
- Don't show attention to another guy or girl while you are on your date.
- Don't be rude to former girlfriends/boyfriends.
- Don't be a know-it-all.
- Don't brag.
- Don't break a date for a better one.
- Don't romanticize about the actors or actresses in a movie.
- Don't be a flirt.
- Don't pout.
- Don't be loud or make a scene.
- Don't criticize your date's choice of friends.
- Don't criticize a former date.
- Don't gossip or betray a confidence.

■■ ■■ ■■

A View of Manners from Bible Days

The Bible contains many love stories, such as Jacob and Rachel and Ruth and Boaz.

Courtship of Ruth and Boaz

The courtship of Ruth and Boaz in the Book of Ruth is a beautiful story. In Ruth 2:4–13, Boaz saw Ruth in the field and asked, "Whose young woman is this?" (v. 5 NASB). And the servants said, "She is the young Moabite woman who returned with Naomi from the land of Moab" (v. 6 NASB). Then Boaz went to where Ruth was gleaning and gathering and said to her, "Listen carefully, my daughter. Do not go to glean in another field; furthermore, do not go on from this one, but stay here with my maids. Let your eyes be on the field which they reap, and go after them. Indeed, I have commanded the servants not to touch you. When you are thirsty, go to the water jugs and drink from what the servants draw" (vv. 8–9 NASB).

Then she fell on her face and asked him why she had found favor in his sight, since she was a foreigner. He told her he had been told all that she had done for her mother-in-law, Naomi, after the death of

Naomi's son and husband. He also pronounced a blessing on her in Ruth 3:10–11: "May you be blessed of the LORD, my daughter. You have shown your last kindness to be better than the first by not going after young men, whether poor or rich. And now, my daughter, do not fear. I will do for you whatever you ask, for all my people in the city know that you are a woman of excellence" (NASB). And to end a beautiful love story, they marry in chapter 4. "So Boaz took Ruth, and she became his wife" (v. 13 NASB).

Chapter 8

Success in Job Interviews and on the Job

Sooner or later almost everyone looks for a job and a paycheck. The way you go about applying for a job can mean success or failure. Remember, you are selling yourself to a prospective employer. The applicant who makes the best impression and has equal qualifications usually gets the job.

From Web sites on-line to employment services that charge a fee, there are many ways to apply for a job today. Job information can be gleaned from ads in the paper, by word of mouth, by asking friends, and by going to job fairs. No matter what route you take, you will need an application and a résumé.

To begin, contact the company or business you are interested in by telephone or letter. If you call, tell the secretary or receptionist that you would like to make an appointment to apply for a job. Get the name of the human resources director or the person in charge of hiring. Make sure you can properly spell and pronounce the names of the people you will be meeting. You can get that information from the human resources director as well.

If you write for an interview, type a brief cover letter giving your education or recent work experience and whether you want part-time or full-time employment. You can end the letter with, "I would like to make an appointment with you to talk about the possibilities of a job with your company. I will call to see when I can schedule an interview." Make sure you send it to the right person.

> *A law firm continues to get mail for Mr. Barker, who founded the firm. He has been dead since 1974, but his name remains on the letterhead.*

The cover letter should make you look competent, indicating that you will be an asset to the company. The first paragraph should attract your prospective employer's interest. Highlight your qualifications and tell how you can use them to benefit the company.

Example:

Mr. Russell Farer
Axion Telecommunications Company
4409 Advent Street
New York, New York 77703

Dear Mr. Farer:

Mr. Harry Swindler suggested that I contact you about the position as manager of your customer service department. My four years experience at TWR, where I was in charge of major accounts, will be valuable in keeping Axion Tele-communications ahead of the competition.

At TWR I received five customer service awards while implementing our division's new 800 service. I feel sure that my experience and my organizational skills will be an asset to Axion Telecommunications.

I would like to make an appointment with you to talk about the possibilities of a job with your company. I will tele-phone to see when I can schedule an interview. You may contact me at 555-0500.

Sincerely,
Barry Owens

The following are from actual cover letters accompanying résumés. They were printed in the July 21, 1997 issue of Fortune *magazine.*

> *"I have an excellent track record, although I am not a horse."*
>
> *"Failed bar exam with relatively high grades."*
>
> *"It's best for employers that I not work with people."*
>
> *"I procrastinate, especially when the task is unpleasant."*
>
> *"Personal interest: donating blood. Fourteen gallons so far."*
>
> *"Please don't misconstrue my 14 jobs as 'job-hopping.' I have never quit a job."*

The Application Blank

Many businesses have application forms for you to complete. Sometimes you can get one over the Internet. You can usually get one by going in person to the personnel office or by writing for one. You may be told to come by the office to pick up a blank form. Get two copies if possible so that you can practice on one before making a final copy. Read the questions carefully and answer them accurately. No matter how insignificant your work experience may appear to you, include it on the form. It will indicate your willingness to work.

There is usually a place for salary requirements. Write "Open" if you don't wish to specify. You will likely discuss salary in a second interview.

Never misrepresent anything. You will be found out. For instance, if you are asked if you have applied there before, admit it. Applications are kept for years by large companies, and reviewers will discover your previous application and any discrepancies between the two when they check their files.

Some high-profile cases in the media have revealed lying from the top of an organization downward, resulting in the demise of the company or corporation. A survey in September 2001 by executive recruitment firm Christian and Timbers found that "23 percent of executives misrepresent their accomplishments." The survey of seven thousand résumés showed that the most common offenses were misstating the number of years in a job and exaggerating achievements. Of course, when such discrepancies are discovered, the people are fired.

Take your own pen, one that you can rely on for neatness. Punctuation, spelling, and good grammar are important. Your application and résumé are permanent impressions of you. If you are using an ink pen, as you should, and you should make a big error in your writing, mark through it with one line and write the corrected wording above it. If you can't write legibly, print.

Applying On-line

The way you submit your résumé should fit the type of job you are seeking. For instance, Ellen Menking, managing director of staffing for human resources consulting firm People Solutions Inc. in Dallas says, "Even the communications method job applicants use can influence the impression they make on a hiring manager. If it's a technology company, they're not all that impressed with things that come through the mail or fax because they don't mess with it, and they might wonder why you are."

She also says that "once you have landed a sit-down interview, don't fire off E-mails every few days afterward. When you're responding to the client, have something of real substance in your E-mail, not just, 'Thanks for the interview. Hope to talk to you again soon.' One substantive E-mail follow-up will be better regarded than repetitive inquiries. An E-mail between each meeting is appropriate, and an E-mail with some substance in it is most appropriate."[1]

According to Cary Welch, senior account manager for Accucom Technical Services Ind., in Richardson, Texas, a high-tech outsourcing firm that works with telecommunications companies, "Information technology job seekers need to be careful that they don't step over the line separating persistence from annoyance."[2]

Joyce Lain Kennedy of the *Dallas Morning News* in her column *Careers* cites some sources of irritation for recruiters. E-stalking is E-mailing your résumé repeatedly. Checking back periodically works best if you send new information of interest to the recruiter. For instance, you might scan and send a brief, relevant news article and add that you continue to look forward to the right timing for an interview.

Another annoyance is what she calls "caps and taps" or "sending E-mails with no use of capitalization whatsoever, or with some words mysteriously capitalized and those that should be—proper names, beginning of a sentence—are not capitalized." E-mails should be as accurate and succinct as other correspondence.

Ms. Kennedy also says that she dislikes "attachments rather than pasting in plain text copy into E-mail for companies that automatically process résumés." Instead, do both. "In addition to enclosing your résumé in plain text within an E-mail, offer the recruiter the option of a more attractively formatted version in an attachment."[3]

Web Sites for Job Hunting

Hendrix College Career Services offers these sites as good resources for career planning and résumé preparation services:

- www.monstertrak.com
- www.monster.com[4]

The Résumé

A résumé is simply an outline of who you are, where you went to school, and when and where you have worked, listing the type of work you did. Your résumé should be kept up-to-date with your work history. If you are just out of school, your educational background should be detailed. Your résumé is the place to list all your accomplishments, honors, awards, and organizational involvement, along with any offices you held within the organization. The people who hire applicants want to see qualities of leadership.

For a fee, professional résumé writers will help you prepare your résumé. Preparation services range from sixty dollars and up. Your résumé should be printed on good quality paper that will hold up so that it can be scanned, faxed, or photocopied. Carry extra copies of your résumé with you to the interview.

Make sure that all the information needed to contact you is at the top of the page. The résumé should include the following information:

- Name
- Address
- Telephone number
- E-mail address
- Education (diplomas or certificates received) honors, awards, courses related to the job you are applying for
- Your interests and hobbies
- Church and civic affiliations
- Past work experience
- Names, addresses, and phone numbers of three people whom you have asked to provide a reference for you

You can ask previous employers, teachers, family friends, and church officials to provide references. Remember you must get their permission to submit their name. Do not give family members as references. Your public library can offer books on different types and styles of résumés. Finally, make sure there are no grammatical or punctuation errors.

Preparing Your Résumé

Hendrix College Career Services suggests these books for help in preparing your résumé:

- *Résumés That Knock 'em Dead* by Martin Yate
- *Adams Résumé Almanac*—Adams Media Corporation
- *High Impact Résumés and Letters* by Ronald L. Krannich, Ph.D. and William J. Banis, Ph.D.

Preparing for the Interview

Your preparation for the interview is as important as the interview. Write down the time, the date, the location with good directions, and the name of the interviewer. Take this information with you. Before the big day, locate the building, parking facilities, and time and distance to travel.

Allow plenty of time to reach the location about thirty minutes early. Do not present yourself in the office more than ten minutes early.

Look the Part

You should be dressed appropriately, and your jewelry (if any) should be understated. Your hair and nails should be clean and well-groomed. Your clothes should be clean and pressed. You should plan to dress a step above the position you are applying for. For instance, if you will be wearing jeans or coveralls on a construction crew, you will want to wear dress slacks, a shirt with a collar, and shoes with a shine for the interview. A tie and conservative sport jacket would complete your professional look. For an office job, wear a suit and tie and dress shoes.

A young lady looks best in a skirt and blouse, suit or tailored dress, hose, and shoes with medium heels and closed toes. Clothes should not be too tight. For business, makeup and hairdo should be understated and not garish. Ask someone with experience to check your appearance for professionalism. (See chapter 5, "Dressing to Achieve")

Know Their Business

Know something about the company—at least what they make or sell. Show you have researched the company and have thought about what you would like them to know about you, as well as what you can contribute to the company or organization. Know the names of the president and chairman of the board. See if they have a newsletter that would give you more information. Check out their Web site. These things show you are interested and that you want to work for them. If appropriate, study their annual report.

The Interview Step-by-Step

You finally have an interview scheduled. Allow yourself plenty of time to reach the location thirty minutes early. Take a copy of your résumé with you so you can refer to it, if needed. Check your appearance just before entering the reception office. Remember that your first impression is the way you look when you walk through the doorway. The receptionist may notice and pass his or her comments on to the interviewer. So don't slouch in and plop on the first available chair thinking you will save your good impression for later.

Enter the office no more than ten minutes early. Confidently give your name to the receptionist and state why you are there and your scheduled time with Mr. or Ms. Interviewer. Wait for the receptionist to give you directions about where to sit and where to put your coat or umbrella if you have one. If no instructions are given, look for a receptacle or a nearby corner where you can stand your wet umbrella. Take your coat with you and place it over the back of your chair. Don't ask what you should do with them. In other words, don't create a problem out of a minor, personal inconvenience such as a hat and coat.

Approach the receptionist with a smile, a firm handshake (if offered), and a businesslike attitude. Don't slink in or shrink back. Be seated where you are told, and don't sit back too comfortably in a plush, overstuffed cushion. You will struggle awkwardly to rise when the time comes to meet the interviewer.

When you are ushered into the interviewer's office, extend your hand as you introduce yourself (remember the six Ss in chapter 2). You can wash your hands with hot water in the rest room before the interview in order to have a warm, dry handshake.

Remain standing until the interviewer sits or asks you to be seated. Keep your posture erect by sitting near the front of the chair. Don't fidget nervously. Hands are always a problem. What to do with them? Relax them in your lap. Women can hold their hands together. Males can rest their hands on their legs. Hands can rest on the arms of the chair or hold a notebook that you brought. Whatever you do, don't bounce one foot on the floor or swing a leg that you have crossed over the other leg.

Be prepared to answer questions directly and concisely. If you are asked, "How are you?" don't give a detailed health report. Simply say, "I'm fine, thank you." Don't become too comfortable.

Be Diplomatic

Let the interviewer ask the questions, but make complete statements. When you answer, don't just grunt with "yeah." In the deep South, it is still appropriate to say, "Yes, sir" and "No, sir," but such responses are not expected in other parts of the country. Stay on the subject and look the interviewer in the eye. Don't exaggerate your abilities and don't belittle them. Honesty and modesty are the best and safest policy. It is easier to remember the truth when you retell it than a lie or made-up story.

A young man applied for a job, saying he had played baseball at a nearby university. When the interviewer called a colleague he knew who also went to that school, he learned that the young man never played on the team. He was the manager.

Typical Questions from the Interviewer

- Did your parents pay all your college fees or did you work to help with expenses?
- Why do you think you can work for this company?

- What skills or abilities do you have that you think would be helpful to you in this job?
- Under what circumstances did you leave your last job?
- What do you think your former employer would have to say about your job performance?

Be prepared to answer some deeper questions suggested by Gary Meyers in "The Meyers Report."

- What are the two most stressful experiences you've had in your life?
- What are the greatest challenges you've faced in your work life? The greatest success? How did each come about and what did you learn?
- What kind of study habits did you have in school? Describe your work style.

According to Nicholas Corcodilos, the director of an executive search and consulting firm, the job interview has evolved into "a hands-on, at-work meeting with an employer who needs to get a job done and a worker who is fully prepared to do the job during the interview. The interviewer may describe a situation and ask the candidate how he or she would handle it. The purpose of this tactic is to watch how the candidate tackles and solves business problems. During this process the candidate should talk about how they have tackled similar assignments in the past and the business tools they bring to work out the solution to the problem."[5]

If you are asked why you want to work there, have some idea of what service you can offer the company. Don't ask what they can do for you. Don't ask about vacation time and coffee breaks. The company is an employer, not a benefactor. When you are asked if you have any questions, be prepared with at least one question such as to whom you would report, about their stock option plan, or about advancement opportunities. Ask about long-term possibilities and opportunities for training. If salary has not been discussed, ask about it now. Before leaving, make a strong, positive statement about your desire for the position: "I am very interested in working here, and I hope you will consider me for the position."

A Good Exit

When the interview is completed, the interviewer may simply say that you will be notified if any positions open up for which you are qualified. When he or she rises, you should rise simultaneously and extend your hand to thank him or her for seeing you. Be sure to call him or her by the proper name and title: Mr. Jones or Professor Wylie. NOTE: Young women and young men shake hands the same. With your hand in a horizontal position and your thumb pointing upward (as though you were going to slap something), slide your hand into the other person's hand until the web between your thumb and forefinger meet. If you go up to the web on the other person's hand, you are not likely to crush the other hand or give a limp handshake.[6]

You should say you are looking forward to hearing from him or her. Exit as you came in, with a smile, even if you are told nothing is available for you. On your way out, thank the receptionist or anyone else who may have helped you upon entering. Don't forget your umbrella.

Write a brief thank-you note immediately. Even if you don't get the job, it will improve your chances of being recommended to another employer and remembered at this company if something comes open in the future. Unless you are told when to inquire about the job, you may call in a few days or a week to ask if the job has been filled.

Follow-up Letter

Writing a thank-you letter will tell the interviewer that you are well-mannered and appreciative. He or she will remember you from among all the others who interviewed for the job.

Thank the interviewer for his or her time and mention your continued interest in the job. Close your letter with a request for further communication.

Example:

Mr. Russell Farer
Axion Telecommunications Company
4409 Advent Street
New York, New York 77703

Dear Mr. Farer:

I appreciate your taking time to meet with me today. I am excited about the possibility of managing your customer service department.

My experience and training at TWR will be of great benefit to me at Axion Telecommunications.

I look forward to hearing from you. Again, I can be reached at 555-0500.

Sincerely,
Barry Owens

Worst Mistakes in Interviewing

- Arriving late.
- Arriving more than one-half hour early.
- Dressing inappropriately.
- Chewing gum, smoking, eating, drinking.
- Bringing along a friend or relative.
- Not being prepared with information about the company.
- Not practicing the interview if this is your first.
- Belittling or exaggerating your accomplishments.
- Asking too many questions or none at all.
- Inquiring about benefits too early.
- Talking about your salary expectations too early.
- Criticizing anyone, especially a former employer.
- Mentioning names of important people to impress the interviewer.
- Looking tired or bored.
- Glancing at your watch.
- Losing your cool.
- Not following instructions or acting impulsively.

On the Job

How to Get Along with Your Boss

- Always be on time.
- Be honest. If you make a mistake, tell your boss. He will find out anyway. Never place blame on someone else.
- Be accurate. Take enough time to do things right. Speed never substitutes for accuracy. At the same time, don't dawdle.
- Be loyal. Don't complain or gossip.
- Be dependable. Don't play sick.
- Be cheerful. Act as though you enjoy your work.

How to Get Along with Other Employees

- Show respect to others.
- Make "please," "thank you," "pardon me," and "I'm sorry" part of your everyday vocabulary. Use them whenever appropriate.
- Keep a quiet, calm demeanor.
- Don't use rough or inappropriate language.
- Don't gossip.
- Borrow things reluctantly and return property promptly and in good shape.

Proper Attire and Grooming for the Business World

The way you dress for the job interview is important, but dressing appropriately on the job is just as important. Consider these common faux pas in business attire:

- Limp, wrinkled clothes
- Short socks that expose the skin when the legs are crossed and you are wearing
- Unpolished shoes or shoes in need of repair
- A tie too short, too long, or too gaudy
- Too many accessories
- Chipped nail polish
- Long fingernails (1/4 inch is long enough)
- Skirts shorter than one inch above the knee
- Loud eye shadow
- Too much makeup
- Patterned or colorful hosiery
- Hair longer than shoulder length not pinned up (Long flowing hair is considered too sexy in the cooperate world.)
- Revealed undergarments
- Open-toed pumps (considered too sexy)
- Hosiery with runs or snags
- Earrings that dangle too long
- Bracelets that jangle
- Bulging pants pockets
- Worn out or ill-fitting belts
- A ring on every finger
- Too many necklaces
- Smudged, dirty eyeglasses
- Soiled clothing
- Clothes with a "pilled" or "nubby" appearance (Synthetic fabrics do this with age.)
- Clothes with missing buttons and loose threads
- Visible underwear lines
- Blouses too sheer or too low cut
- A slip that shows through the slit in a skirt
- Clothes that show too much skin (Long sleeves are best for men.*)
- Clothes with inappropriate slogans or sayings
- Bra or slip strap showing or falling off the shoulder

---

*In the deep South, during the summer, men may wear short-sleeved shirts to work in some offices, and women may wear sleeveless blouses.

- Not using a lint brush
- Unbuttoned buttons and unzipped zippers
- Neckline tags showing at the back of the neck
- Not wearing a camisole under see-through blouses or shirts
- An overblouse or shirt that is too short when the arms are raised
- Not wearing proper leg wear (hosiery** or trouser socks)
- Wearing knee-high hosiery with skirts

Improper Grooming

- Facial hair—beard, nose, ears, or brows—untrimmed
- Clipping nails in public
- Chewing gum or using a toothpick in public
- Manicuring in public
- Dressing for fad or current trend in fashion rather than appropriate business style
- Applying makeup in public
- Women wearing their hair in their face
- Not brushing teeth and tongue privately after lunch
- Wearing too much perfume or cologne

General Bad Habits

- Using poor grammar and slang
- Not listening attentively
- Cutting in line
- Biting your fingernails
- Interrupting
- Breaking a promise or commitment without good cause or explanation
- Not helping when someone drops something
- Not opening doors for others
- Not answering an RSVP
- Not delivering a message
- Dropping by someone's office or home unexpectedly
- Embarrassing someone by publicly calling attention to a flaw (slip showing or zipper unzipped)
- Showing jealous tendencies
- Asking to borrow someone's makeup or comb
- Not thanking someone who opens a door for you
- Cracking your knuckles
- Being loud and obnoxious

**In the deep South, during the summer, some companies may allow women to refrain from wearing hose.

According to the Melton Leadership System, dealing with people is an important day-to-day challenge. Research indicates that about 15 percent of one's financial and career success is due to technical skills while the remaining 85 percent is due to people skills, the ability to work effectively with and get along with others.[7]

> *A company president took one of his young executives to lunch one day for the first time. Purpose: to tell him he was to be sent to Paris to run the small branch office there. It was a plum of a job. The president ruefully reported afterward that "by the time this young man had dipped his napkin in his water glass in order to wipe his mouth, and said, 'Gimme' three times to the waiter while ordering his food, I knew this guy was not going to represent us in Paris."[8]*

■■ ■■ ■■

A View of Manners from Bible Days

Various occupations are named in Scripture such as carpenter (Joseph), hunter (Esau), farmer (Boaz), merchant (Lydia), tax collector (Zacheus), doctor (Luke), and fishermen (Peter, James, and John).

Miriam and the Princess

In the story of Miriam and Moses in the bulrushes, we have a job interview where Miriam applied for her mother to work for the Pharoah's princess. In Exodus 2, we see Miriam asking the daughter of Pharaoh, "Shall I go and call a nurse for you from the Hebrew women, that she may nurse the child for you?" (v. 7 NASB).

In chapter 1, we read that Pharaoh had commanded all his people to cast all boy babies into the Nile, killing every son who was born. Moses' mother was afraid for her young son, so she hid him in the bulrushes, and she set Miriam to watch over him. When the princess came to bathe, Miriam approached her with her question. The princess answered, "'Go ahead.' So the girl went ahead and called the child's mother" (Exod. 2:8 NASB).

Jesus the Carpenter

Our Lord, the King of Kings, the Messiah, was a carpenter by trade. He didn't have to have an occupation, but he trained with his earthly father so He would have a job. He was no loafer.

In Mark 6, we see Jesus going back to his hometown of Nazareth "to teach in the synagogue, and many who heard Him were astonished"

(v. 2). They began to ask questions like "'Where did this man get these things [wise teachings]? . . . Isn't this the carpenter?' . . . So they were offended by Him" (vv. 2–3).

Bankers and Lenders

An interesting occupation in the Bible is banker. The Phoenicians invented the money-lending system, and it was in full operation in the various provinces of the Roman Empire in Christ's time. The law of Moses did not allow the Israelites to lend to one another, charging interest (Deut. 23:19ff NASB). But it did allow them to charge interest on loans made to Gentiles (Deut. 23:20 NASB). Jesus did not condemn the charging of interest by a bank, because he used the word *usury*, meaning "interest".[9]

Jesus said, "But his master replied to him, 'You . . . should have deposited my money with the bankers. And when I returned I would have received my money back with interest'" (Matt. 25:26–27).

Chapter 9

RSVP and Personal Correspondence

Electronic communication is a wonderful new convenience, especially E-mail, faxes, and cell phones; but an electronic message cannot take the place of a handwritten note. Taking time to pen a short note or letter will do more to help you leave a favorable, lasting impression than you may realize. And it's not really that difficult if you have the right tools and learn a few rules. When you take the time and effort to write a thank-you note, bread-and-butter note (after an overnight visit), informal invitation and reply, congratulatory note, introduction, condolence, or any other sentiment, you give the recipient something tangible to savor. All of the above should be handwritten. If you purchase a card or generate one on your computer with printed words inside, add a few handwritten words of your own before signing it.

The Tools

Whether you order engraved or printed stationery with your name or initials or if you buy simple, plain fold-over notes in a box, you should always have them easily accessible with a good pen and a roll of stamps. Keeping your address book in the same place is useful, also.

The Stationery

Engraved or printed stationery is ordered in a stationery store, a gift shot, or any other business that stocks such items. A box of notes that we often call thank-you notes can usually be found in any grocery, discount, or upscale department store. Remember that the more you pay, the better the grade of paper you get. Preferred are the heavy envelopes that don't expose the handwriting of your notes inside.

Look through the store's catalogs for paper, style, fonts, and personalized samples of initials, called monograms, or address imprinting.

> *Monograms were created for stationery hundreds of years ago for illiterate members of royalty to authorize documents and proclamations. Charlemagne was one of the early users of monograms. He was unable to write his name, so he drew his monogram in lieu of signing his name.*[1]
>
> —*Crane's Blue Book of Stationery*

Another form of appropriate paper is a heavy card with a corresponding envelope. These are called correspondence cards and are a good choice to use in business. They are flat, heavy cards that are used for brief messages and notes. Your name may be imprinted at the top of the card. The envelope may show your name and address on the back flap.

The size varies, but it is usually about four by five inches or seven by ten inches, though other dimensions are fine. You may want to get your cards monogrammed or personalized in some way, but it is not necessary. For serious correspondence, gray, white, or beige paper is the best color. A pen with blue or black ink is most appropriate. Other colors of ink are less than formal and should not be used for most communication. All formal correspondence, such as wedding invitations, should be printed or engraved in black ink only.

Boxed notes may be imprinted on the front of the fold-over note with either your name or your initials but without any titles. These are good for business or social uses.

If you use sheets of stationery, they are folded once and put in the envelope by placing the open edges in first. These sheets can be imprinted at the top with your name only or with your name and address. All stationery is inserted into the envelope so that the recipient can remove it from the flap side of the envelope in the easiest-to-read manner.

Writing the Note or Letter

Hand-write the date on the lower left-hand side (inside for fold-over notes). Otherwise, you may place the date at the upper right-hand side of the first page.

The salutation is written on the left side of the letter, followed by the body with indented paragraphs, and the closing and signature on the right side.

Good complimentary closings for social notes include: Sincerely, Yours cordially, Affectionately yours, Regretfully, or some form of these. In business, good choices are: Yours truly, Yours respectfully, Sincerely yours, and Cordially.

Paper has been a part of civilization since the Egyptians developed a paper-like substance called papyrus *four thousand years ago. (Our word* paper *is derived from* papyrus.*) Papyrus is a reed that grows along the banks of the Nile. Called bulrushes in the Bible, they were the reeds in which Moses was hidden from Pharoah.*[2]

—Crane's Blue Book of Stationery

Good Points to Remember

Never begin a letter or note with an apology. Mention your regrets in the body or conclusion of the letter. Use a dictionary to check your spelling. Read the note aloud to see if it is easy to read and makes sense. Wait a few hours or a day, then read it again to be sure you want to mail it. Avoid underscoring, exclamation points, using all capital letters, or postscripts. It's always better to write words out rather than use abbreviations or symbols. For example, January instead of Jan., suite for ste, drive for dr.

Do not write on both sides of the paper. Such letters are hard to read. An exception is the fold-over note. You may finish your message on the back. Begin at the inside top of a fold-over note if there is no monogram or embossing on the front. Both monogramming and embossing leave indentations on the inside, and your writing will be uneven. Begin writing just below the fold on this type of note.

A thank-you note should be sent within one week after receiving a gift, favor, or invitation. Exceptions include large weddings where hundreds of notes are to be written and mailed. Family members deserve a written thank-you even if you don't mail it, but decide to put it on their pillow or the breakfast table.

When you have been a guest at a dinner or a party, address your note to the lady of the house, but mention the husband in the body of the letter. Sign both your first and last names. Mail it to the home. Don't make them guess which "Tom" you are.

Avoid buying notes that have "Thank you" printed on the front. They become redundant when you write a thank-you note inside.

The Bread-and-Butter or Hospitality Note

When you have been an overnight guest or a weekend guest, you should write a bread-and-butter note within a few days of your stay. This note does not differ from the thank-you note except in the wording. Address it to the hostess. The same type note can be written after a dinner party. Notice the punctuation and format for social correspondence.

Dear Carla,

Your hospitality made me feel so much at home and made my stay in your home one I will long remember. The activities and the plans you had for the weekend were my favorite kinds of things to do. You are a superb cook as well.

Thank you for a wonderful weekend.

Sincerely,
(Signature of first and last names)
(Date)

A Thank-you Note for a Gift

Mail this handwritten note within a week, if possible. Identify the gift and tell how you plan to use it. A verbal thank-you is not enough. Send a written note as well.

Dear Kelly,

I want to thank you for the lovely picture frame you gave me for my birthday. You chose just the right size to fit on my entry table. I will display it with pride.

I appreciate your thoughtfulness.

Sincerely,
(Signature of first and last names)
(Date)

A Note of Sympathy

Keep the bereaved person in mind when you write this note. If you knew the deceased, mention something nice that you remember about the person. If you know only the one you are writing, express your sorrow for his or her loss.

Dear Mrs. Fontaine:

The news of the death of your father came as quite a shock. I remember him as such a robust man. I want to tell you how sorry I am to learn of your loss.

I would like to help in any way I can during this difficult time. Please let me know.

Sincerely,
(Signature of first and last names)
(Date)

Invitations and Replies

> *Wedding invitations were once engraved with oil-based inks. These inks were very slow to dry, so tissue was inserted between the invitations to prevent smudging. Etiquette once called for removing the tissue, since it was just packing material and served no purpose.*
>
> *However, many people failed to remove the tissue, and, through usage, tissued wedding invitations became acceptable and eventually were considered elegant. Today, most inks are water-based and dry rapidly. Tissuing is not necessary anymore, but it has become so associated with elegance and good taste that it is now considered proper.[3]*
>
> *—Crane's Blue Book of Stationery*

No matter how formal or informal, always acknowledge an invitation within a week of receiving it. Your answer must not be maybe or perhaps but yes or no. You should abide by your decision unless there is a death in the family or you become ill. Some people mistakenly think that if they are not going to attend they need not reply.

> *In New Testament times invitations were issued in two stages: a first, formal request was always refused with thanks (which added ritual stature to the guest). There followed, if the host really wanted to pursue the matter, a much more urgent and personal badgering; eventually the guest might allow his or her resistance to crumble. An example is the hospitality offered Paul and his friends by Lydia, the dealer in purple textiles, in the Acts of the Apostles. She first asked them, then "constrained" them, or, as we still say, "prevailed upon" them.[4]*
>
> *—Margaret Visser, The Rituals of Dinner*

How you reply depends on the instructions on the invitation. The abbreviation RSVP stands for the French words *Répondez, s'il vous plaît.* They mean, "Please respond," and you must. If the invitation states "regrets only" it is necessary to reply only if you are not going to attend. You will definitely be expected at the appointed time if you do not respond. If a phone number is given, you may telephone your answer; but if there is no phone number, you are expected to write your answer. Envelopes and plain, blank cards, fold-over notes, or small sheets of paper with no lines are appropriate.

For a dinner, a handwritten invitation should be mailed three weeks in advance. The response to that invitation should come within a week.

> *Through usage new customs become a part of our etiquette. Reply cards were once considered improper, insulting, and horrendous. Wedding invitations were always answered in one's own handwriting on one's own stationery. Today, the majority of wedding invitations are sent with reply cards. They are being used because they are filling a new need.*[5]
>
> —*Crane's Blue Book of Stationery*

Addressing the Envelope

You may have your complete address without your name printed or engraved on the back flap or on the front, left corner. The postal machines scan the mail at the post office more efficiently when you put it in the upper left corner.

To distinguish social correspondence from business writing, indent each line of the address. For example:

_____

    _____

       _____

In business, the address is flush with the left margin. For example:

_____

_____

_____

Titles and Names

Your own personal supply of stationery makes a nice gift that you may want to request. If you choose printed or engraved (more expensive) cards or sheet paper, have your initials or full name placed across the top (no title). For business cards, men and women may put a title after their name. Men always have their initials in a straight line. Thomas Allen

Bowers would be TAB in block letters. If you are a junior, the second, or the third, you will want to have your name printed this way: Thomas Allen Bowers Jr. (or Junior); Thomas Allen Bowers II; or Thomas Allen Bowers III. (Nephews are named II, while a son is named Junior.) Partial initials are not appropriate, such as Thomas A. Bowers. If you go to a reputable stationery business, you usually will be instructed concerning the best choices of paper, ink, form, and content.

Unmarried women place their initials as follows: Mary Ann Brown would be M A B with Brown as the last name, or M B A. The middle initial stands for the last name and is usually in larger typeface. "Titles of courtesy have no place either in a signature or on a personal card."[6] Exceptions are Mr. and Mrs. on a personal gift card or when a woman has a good reason for designating her marital status. For example, Jeanette Stapler (Mrs. Ralph Stapler).

A young man is addressed as "Master" until he is about seven years old. From seven until age eighteen, he is addressed without a title. Then he becomes Mr. whereas a woman is addressed as "Miss" from birth. Women who never marry usually adopt the Ms. title to replace Miss after they are about twenty-five, unless they prefer to keep Miss. After age twenty-five, she adopts Ms. or continues to use Miss unless she marries.

A married or widowed woman is addressed socially using her husband's name: Mrs. Robert Anderson. A widowed woman continues to use her husband's first name, but a divorced woman does not. The divorcée may replace her former husband's first name with her first name or with her maiden name. For example, Mrs. Sims Barber, with Sims as her maiden name, or Ms. Janis Barber, with Janis as her first name. Of course, some divorcées take their maiden name back legally. In that case, her name would be Ms. Janis Sims again. Tip: If you don't know if the woman is Miss, Mrs., or Ms., use Ms. It conveniently addresses any woman.

Never put a title both before and after a name with the exception of titles like Junior or Jr.; therefore, Mr. John Smith Jr. is correct. You may use Mr. and Mrs. for a married couple. When writing a professional man or woman use "Mr.," "Dr.," etc., or simply their full name followed by their professional title: Aaron Murry Ambrose, M.D. Never write or type Dr. Aaron Murry Ambrose, M.D.

Social correspondence and formal invitations should be addressed by hand in black ink. Computer labels, word processor addresses, or stick-on address labels are sometimes acceptable in business but not for social notes such as wedding invitations, announcements, or greeting cards. All notes and letters should be mailed in a stamped envelope rather than in a metered one. If you are invited to a home wedding or a reception (including or excluding the wedding ceremony), you should reply within a week, giving your intentions.

Gift enclosure cards were called visiting cards before the telephone. They are about one and one-half by three inches in size. They have envelopes, but are too small to mail. Today you can use them as enclosures for gifts, or you may write on them and leave someone a brief note.

In formal correspondence, it is better to spell out titles such as Doctor or The Honorable.

Someone other than the titled individual uses titles such as Mr., Mrs., Ms., Miss, Doctor, and The Honorable. In other words, don't sign papers using your title. Simply sign Carl Stack, not Mr. Carl Stack, and not The Honorable Mr. Stack.

How (Not) to Use English Properly

"Exaggeration is a billion times worse than understatement."
"Proofread carefully to see if you any words out."
"Puns are for children, not groan readers."
"Also, always avoid annoying alliteration."
"Also, too, never, ever use repetitive redundancies."
"One-word sentences? Eliminate."
"No sentence fragments."

A View of Manners from the Bible

For correspondence we have only to look at the epistles of Paul in the New Testament for good examples. Paul's letters, written to the churches and to his associates such as Timothy, are treasures to us today.

Invitations

We also have examples of invitations in Jesus' time. In Bible times, "the one invited must not at first accept, but is expected rather to reject the invitation. He must be *urged* to accept. Although all the time he expects to accept".[7]

After she and her household were baptized, she urged us, "If you consider me a believer in the Lord, come and stay at my house." And she persuaded us (Acts 16:15).

Chapter 10

Telecommunications

When Alexander Graham Bell invented the technology for instant communication, he gave us a lifesaving tool that connects us to the world. From his ingenuity, we have progressed to cell phones, fax machines, beepers, electronic mail, and various other devices. These complex instruments make our lives more convenient and at the same time more complicated. Without a new code of electronic manners to guide us through the maze of instruments available for our use, we can get into all kinds of trouble.

With our voice alone, we make a first impression on telephone equipment perhaps more often than we do in person. We often communicate with people who will never see our face. Therefore, our tone of voice, our facial expressions, and our energy level are all important. Our body language is useless. We can't make eye contact or nod in agreement. We are easily distracted, and the person on the other end of the line will know we are not paying attention.

Telephone Etiquette

Probably 75 to 76 percent of today's business is conducted on the telephone. Who knows how much of our personal life is spent talking on the phone? Habits are hard to break, but developing good telephone etiquette is worth the boost you will give your self-image and the good image you will project.

Practice these courteous telephone tips, and they will become habit:

Making a call

- Smile as you begin to speak on the phone whether you are receiving or making a call. Use a mirror if necessary to check your appearance. A smile can be heard in your voice.

- Always identify yourself with your first and last names. It's rude to say, "Guess who this is."
- If you are unsure you have reached the correct number, you may ask, "Have I reached . . . ?" and give the number.
- If you recognize the voice of the person who answers the phone, speak to him or her by name after you have identified yourself.
- Ask for the person you wish to speak to and say please and thank you.
- Wait quietly. Don't sing, hum, or strum your fingers. The person who picks up the receiver on the other end will hear you.
- Always take the time of day into consideration when you make a call. After 10:00 P.M. is usually too late to call unless there is an emergency.
- Always ask if this is a convenient time for your friend (or business person) to talk. If it is not, offer to call back.
- Don't eat, drink, chew gum, or talk to others in the room with you. Give your phone partner your full attention.
- Keep your phone call brief. Others may be waiting to use the phone.
- If you need to use someone else's phone, always ask permission and offer to pay the toll charges if there are any.
- Use courtesy words like *please* and *thank you*.
- When you place the call, you are the one to say good-bye first, after making sure the other person has finished talking. Never say, "Bye-bye." Say, "Good-bye." In business, the client or customer says good-bye first. When a telephone connection is broken, the caller should replace the call.
- When you reach a wrong number, do not hang up before saying, "I am sorry," or, "Sorry, I must have the wrong number."
- Always close on a positive note. Your last words and your tone of voice are what people take away from your conversation.

Answering the Telephone

Concentrate on having a pleasant voice and answering with a smile. Listen carefully when the caller gives you his or her name so you can remember and use it. If the call is not for you and you must get someone else to the phone, ask the caller if he or she can wait while you get the person to the phone. Quietly lay the receiver down and notify the person that he or she has a call. Don't shout.

If the person asked for is not available, ask if you may take a message. Taking a message is important if the person is not there to receive the call. Always have pen and paper by the phone. Write down messages carefully. Think about how you would want a message taken down for you.

Answering Machines

> *"Hi. I'm probably here. I'm just avoiding someone I don't like. Leave me a message, and if I don't call back, it's you."* A message on an answering machine as reported in the Arkansas Democrat-Gazette, 8 October 1997.

About 60 percent of Americans have answering machines in their homes. With the number of home businesses on the rise, business people often have a voice mailbox with more options as an extension of their home answering machine. Callers find it frustrating to wade through a long list of options, but people who offer the options find it hard to operate without them. A few manners will help.

- Set the machine for four or fewer rings, if possible.
- The outgoing message should be as brief as possible, but give the necessary information. The message most appropriate is, "You have reached 555-0000. Please leave your name, number, and a brief message after the tone."
- You may add that you will return the call as soon as possible, if you plan to do so. Of course, you should make every effort to return calls within twenty-four hours.
- The message should never be cute or contain jargon the caller may not understand. It is not necessary to tell the caller you are unavailable; that is obvious. Leaving a song for the caller to listen to is considered inconsiderate by some, not to mention annoying.

Leaving a Message

State your name and the name of the person you are calling. Give the day and time of your call and briefly summarize the reason for your call. Leave your telephone number with the area code if you ask for a return call.

Say your number slowly. It is difficult to understand a rapid flow of numbers. Don't leave confidential, vague, or mysterious messages. Practical joke messages are inappropriate. Someone else may take the message and misinterpret your intent. Finally, don't assume your message will reach the person you are calling. Machines malfunction and messages get erased.

Receiving a Call

The same courteous rules apply when you answer your phone. Smile and answer with a pleasant tone, not as though you are angry with someone, although you may be. Don't blurt out, "Who is this?" if the caller does not identify himself or herself. Say, "May I ask who is calling?"

Call-Waiting

Call-waiting can be advantageous when you are expecting an important call because you can, early into your conversation, tell the person you are talking to that you are expecting an urgent call and you may have to answer it.

You can also choose to ignore the beep and say, "I have call-waiting, but I'm not going to interrupt our call. Please continue." Never leave a first caller for more than twenty seconds to answer the call-waiting signal unless there is an emergency.

Electronic Mail

Cyberspace presents a vast opportunity to send your messages in an instant anywhere in the world. Electronic mail (E-mail) gives you convenience, multiple addressing, speed, and documentation of your communication. You can type a few words on a computer, and a modem transmits the message over telephone lines to the recipient's computer or other computer equipment. The addressee retrieves the E-mail.

Making a good impression on the Internet means you must abide by some rules.

Netiquette is a set of rules for proper behavior when interacting with people on-line:

- Grammar and spelling are just as important as in a paper copy of your message.
- Use spell check and grammar check if necessary.
- Read your message carefully to avoid leaving out words.
- Avoid jargon and slang.
- Remember that you may send your message in private, but more than a few eyes may see it.
- For serious communication fill in the subject line carefully and formally—nothing cute.
- Begin each message on a positive note. Save your complaint for later or not at all.
- Don't make jokes or funny remarks that might be offensive. If you feel that a member of your family would be embarrassed by reading your message, don't send it.

- You may find comfort in thinking your words can be easily deleted, but your words may be saved on the other end and cause you great difficulty later.
- E-mail offers no privacy. Even the signature block is there for everyone to read. In some states E-mail messages are admitted as evidence in a courtroom.
- Don't type words in all caps because the readers feel you are shouting at them. To emphasize a word enclose it in stars, * . . . . *
- Double-check the TO: and CC: lines because once the message is sent, it cannot be easily retrieved, if at all.
- Write only what you would say to the person face-to-face. Impulsive, reactive E-mail users rudely produce flame mail. Flame mail is inappropriate and consists of personal insults or expressions of strong opinion. It is sometimes called hate mail.
- The term *spamming* describes unwanted, irrelevant messages. The term comes from the name of the canned-meat product, SPAM, which is a hodgepodge of many different meat products. Electronic spamming wastes time and space.
- Send only E-mail messages that you would freely put on a post-card for anyone to see.

The Internet

The Internet is a communications service to which you can sub-scribe. No matter who supplies the Internet access—an Internet service provider, a university, or a corporation—these organizations have regu-lations about ownership of mail and files and what is proper to send. Ask about the rules if you are not instructed before you use it.

Laws about the ownership of E-mail vary from place to place, but it is always important to respect the copyright on materials you use. It is illegal to send chain letters in cyberspace. Don't send unsolicited mail asking for information on people whose names you happen to see on a mailing list.

It's a good idea to include the header information at the end of your message. (Sometimes this information is lost.) The signature line at the bottom should not exceed four lines. It makes sure the recipient knows who you are.

Electronic Ethics

Cyberspace allows you to remain faceless. Therefore, some users are tempted to send rude remarks or subtle innuendoes. Do no harm. Instead, send a compliment if deserved.

Ask the following questions before sending E-mail:
* Is the message clear, containing no double meanings?
* Is the wording tasteful?
* Are grammar and spelling correct?
* Have I included encouragement or a pat on the back when appropriate?

Fax Machines

More and more homeowners have fax machines today. You should know how to use one. A fax (facsimile) machine transmits a document through the phone lines to another facsimile machine. The receiver on the other end prints it out. Long-distance charges apply as with a telephone call.

A document to be faxed should include the following: cover sheet, date, name of the sender, sender's fax number and telephone number, name and fax number of the recipient, page count (including the cover page), and a brief message or explanation of the faxed material to follow.
* Send only pertinent information. Junk faxes are never welcome.
* Send only information that is not confidential or controversial. Many eyes may see whatever you send.
* Don't use the fax machine as a substitute for the mail. Stamped, personal notes written by hand on nice paper are more appropriate for saying thanks or congratulations and for sending condolence messages.
* Respect the time and resources of the recipient of any fax. The employee or client receiving the fax provides the paper, employee time, and the machine. Make all your faxes succinct and in good taste.
* Do not use the fax machine to send a last-minute invitation. You appear disorganized and rude.

Laptop Computers

Before using your laptop, consider the tranquility of those around you. The constant clicking of the keyboard can be annoying to those around you on an airplane, for instance. Your cotravelers may feel trapped in a chamber of clatter. It's kind to ask if your typing annoys them.

Cell Phones, Beepers, and Pagers

According to the Cellular Telecommunications Industry Association, the number of wireless phone users in the U.S. alone has exceeded sixty million. Once a status symbol, a cell phone today tells your companions that there is something more important than being with them when you talk on your cell phone. If you are expecting an important call, tell the friends you are with about it at the beginning. Then excuse yourself for as brief a time as possible.

Turn off your cell phone, beeper, or pager or put it on vibrate when you are in most enclosed public spaces such as restaurants, churches, auditoriums, performances, and any place where other people will be disturbed. It's annoying to others to be forced to listen to one side of a conversation, not to mention the noisy disturbance you make.

Home telephone rules apply to cell phone use as well, such as identifying yourself when you make a call. When you have passengers in your car and you must answer or use your mobile phone, be brief and return to your friends or associates as soon as possible.

Avoid putting wireless phone users on hold, because using a cell phone is usually an expense to the owner. Don't ask to use someone's cell or car phone unless it is an emergency.

While car phones are valuable tools, they can hinder safe driving. However, they also give us immediate access to emergency assistance for ourselves or someone else. The following are some recommended tips for safer driving:

- Use a hands-free phone or a speakerphone.
- Use the memory dialing functions to minimize the potential for distraction.
- Dial a number only when you are stopped, or ask a passenger to dial for you.
- Never try to take notes or look up a number while driving. Pull off the road.
- Let your voice mail pick up your calls when it is unsafe to answer the car phone.
- Suspend car telephone conversations when driving conditions become hazardous.

Long-winded Callers

When it is difficult to end a conversation with someone, try some of these tips:

- If you place the call: "I won't take up any more of your time. I'll get right on the project. Good-bye."
- "I'll get back to you right away," or, "Thank you for calling, John."
- "I wish I could talk longer, but I have an appointment. Could we finish this conversation at a later time?"

■■ ■■ ■■

A View of Manners from Bible Days

Whether we are communicating face-to-face or by modern technology such as by telephone, E-mail, or telegram, we should choose our words carefully, passing through the filter of prayer before uttering them.

May the words of my mouth and the meditation of my heart be acceptable to You, O LORD, my rock and my Redeemer (Ps. 19:14).

Your speech should always be gracious, seasoned with salt, so that you may know how you should answer each person (Col. 4:6).

If anyone thinks he is religious, without controlling his tongue but deceiving his heart, his religion is useless (James 1:26).

The Tongue Can Be a Good Thing

When the Lord returns, the following Scriptures will be fulfilled:

For it is written: As I live, says the Lord, every knee will bow to Me, and every tongue will give praise to God (Rom. 14:11).

And every tongue should confess that Jesus Christ is Lord, to the glory of God the Father (Phil. 2:11).

Christians should be prepared: Always be ready to give a defense [answer] to anyone who asks you a reason for the hope that is in you. However, do this with gentleness and respect, keeping your conscience clear, so that when you are accused, those who denounce your Christian life will be put to shame (1 Pet. 3:15–16).

Chapter 11

Weekend or Overnight Guest

Being a host can be as much fun as being a guest if you know how to do it. One word comes to mind when you consider what a gracious host does. That word is *anticipate*. As a host you should foresee all the needs of your guest. For instance, anticipate that your guest will want to know which activities are planned so he or she will pack the right clothes. Being a well-remembered host requires simple thoughtfulness.

Being a Good Host

Pretend you are a guest in your own house. Go through the motions of meeting other family members or roommates, unpacking your clothes, securing an extra blanket, finding the bath linens when it comes time to bathe, checking to see if there is plenty of toilet tissue on the holders, and any other ordinary duties common to daily living. You will want to show your guests the layout of the house so they can get around comfortably without fearing they will enter someone's private domain.

Any time you have guests in your home, unless you are serving a meal soon, offer a light beverage or snack. Always offer to take a guest's coat, hat, suitcase, umbrella, and the like. If your guest is staying overnight, put the luggage in a secure, easy-to-get-to place where it will not mar the furniture or coverings.

Before the visitors come, ask if they have any special needs or if there are certain foods they do not eat. Don't ask the reasons for their likes and dislikes. Try to accommodate your guests in every way you can by asking questions that will make them feel at home.

Sometimes your plans as host go awry. When they do, continually expressing your distress or embarrassment will make your guests uncomfortable. Talking about disasters or fiascos will usually do nothing to ease the situation. If the guest causes a mishap, quickly reassure him, do what you can to right the situation, and graciously accept his apology. An awkward situation calls for a generous, kindhearted response.

If you discover at mealtime that you are serving your guests something they cannot abide, don't embarrass them by repeatedly apologizing and calling attention to the objectionable dish. See that your guests are served something they prefer. They will be forever grateful, not to mention happily satisfied gastronomically.

Plan activities for the visit around the likes and preferences of your guests. Avoid activities you know they do not care for. For instance, if you learn that a particular guest is afraid of heights, don't plan a trip to the tallest building in your city. If you discover such a fear after guests arrive, simply have a back-up plan in mind.

As a host, you are responsible for entertaining and attending to the needs of your guests, whatever that means. You are not permitted to make plans on your own, leave your guests to take care of themselves, or "turn them over" to another family member while you go your own way.

When your guests depart, you want to feel that you treated them the same way you would like to be treated. The Golden Rule is the operative phrase when you have houseguests, as in all areas of life.

What if you are the host once removed; that is, you live in the house, but your roommate or a parent is the primary host? You should greet any guest with a warm welcome. Show enthusiasm as you practice the Ss explained in chapter 2. Be prepared to engage in polite conversation, taking your cue to leave from the host by watching for signs that you have said enough.

Being a Good Guest

The basics of being a good weekend houseguest are detailed in *Emily Post's Guests and Hosts:*

First, you, as a young person, stand when your friend's mother enters the room for the first time. You wait for her to extend her hand to you; you do not offer to shake hands with her first. You are courteous and quiet during quiet times. You offer to help with everything from carrying grocery bags to clearing the table after dinner. You make your bed in the morning, you keep your feet and shoes off the furniture and bedspread, you do not make telephone calls without asking first and paying for them, and you are kind to any siblings your friend may have, even if he or she isn't particularly kind to them herself. You also should keep in mind that your roommate's mother would more than likely appreciate some alone time with her son or daughter, so you make yourself scarce every now and then, pleading studying, a letter to write or the desire to take a walk around the block or into town. If you accomplish all these thoughtful goals, you will surely be a welcome guest again and again.[1]

Some Guidelines for Being a Good Guest

There are a few basic principles you should always remember and implement when you are an overnight guest in someone's home.

- Take your personal toilet articles so you will not have to borrow. If you are going to the beach, take a beach towel.
- Take an inexpensive gift such as food or decorative soaps, or plan to send a small gift after you leave. It should not be expensive. It must not be too personal such as bath powder or perfume.
- Be prepared to do whatever the host has planned. If you have allergies or phobias, you can discreetly mention these to the host privately.
- Be neat. Don't scatter your clothing and other personal items. Take a plastic bag to store your dirty clothes. Hang your used towels on the rack; don't leave them on the floor.
- If you become hungry, you may ask for a snack if it isn't too close to meal time.
- Respect others' privacy. Do not open drawers or snoop in closets.
- When you leave, pack all that you brought. Do not leave something behind that the host must bring or send to you.
- Never leave abruptly. Find the host or hosts and thank them for inviting you, and if possible, say you had a good time.
- Write a thank-you note and leave it there or write one in a few days and mail it. If you had a miserable time, you can always thank the host or hosts for their hospitality.

> *Guests should be well fed, but some may be difficult to satisfy. The following is a humorous story of a guest with a ferocious appetite.*

Several years ago our college son brought his roommate, a football lineman, home for the weekend. I fixed a pound of bacon and a dozen eggs for breakfast the next morning. My husband thanked the Lord for the food, picked up the platter holding the eggs and bacon and passed it to our guest. The young man moved his plate, placed the platter in front of him and began to eat. My husband was speechless. I quickly filled in, 'Don't worry, we have another pound of bacon and another dozen eggs.' I hurriedly fixed them and everyone else got to eat.[2]

A View of Manners from Bible Days

Hospitality was important in New Testament times because there were no motels or hotels and only a few inns. In Bible times people believed that a person who became their guest was sent to them by God. They looked on their duties in the role of host as a sacred duty.

Even today, "If parties of travelers are not too many in number, they will be entertained at a Bedouin tent encampment, or in a village guest room."

In the Old Testament, when Abraham entertained three strangers who proved to be angels, he must have thought heaven had sent him guests (Gen. 18:2-7). He ran to meet the three men, hastened into the tent of Sarah to get her to cook a meal, and then ran to his herd and picked a calf that he hurriedly dressed.[3]

Hospitality of the Shunammite Woman

Second Kings 4:8-37 records the beautiful story of hospitality involving Elisha and the Shunammite woman. When Elisha passed through Shunem, he always stopped at a particular couple's house where they graciously prepared him a meal. One day the wife said to her husband, "Behold now, I perceive that this is a holy man of God passing by us continually. Please, let us make a little walled upper chamber (a weatherproof room on the flat roof of the house) and let us set a bed for him there, and a table and a chair and a lampstand; and it shall be, when he comes to us, that he can turn in there" (vv. 9-10 NASB).

After that Elisha always had the little upper chamber the couple built for him where he could go to eat and sleep. Perhaps we can learn true hospitality from this story for our own day.[4]

Chapter 12

Recreation and Sports

Steel loses its strength when it loses its temper.—An old adage

Every rule of etiquette has a reason behind it. The rules of any game, sport, or recreation have etiquette rules and reasons. The reasons are usually easy to see. Safety and courtesy are obviously required at any sporting activity, or there is no game. Rules prevent chaos and provide direction, guidance, and structure.

Of course, the Golden Rule is once again the primary guiding principle. Players should do for others what they would like done for themselves when their turn comes.

Seattle's Cameron remembers manners: "With four home runs in the (baseball) game already and a chance to break the record, Mike Cameron (of the Seattle Mariners) chose to follow baseball decorum instead. That's the kind of guy he is. . . . When Chicago's Mike Porzio (of the Chicago White Sox) threw three consecutive balls in a 15–4 game, Cameron let a hittable pitch go by for strike one, following the age-old practice of not swinging at a 3–0 pitch in a blowout."[1]

All Sports

Some rules of safety and courtesy that all players should observe apply to all recreation, whether on the golf course, tennis court, or some other field of play.

- Always arrive on time, early if possible, and ready to play. If you have an emergency and must cancel, get another player to take your place.

- If you must cancel, let the appropriate people know as soon as possible.
- Upon arrival, greet each player cordially with a handshake and a smile.
- Make sure your attire is proper for a particular sport or club in the area. The correct shoes are extremely important in sports such as golf, basketball, and tennis.
- Do not fake knowing how to play the game. You may appear foolish later. Take lessons, read up on the sport, or ask someone for help.
- Never pretend to be better at any sport than you really are.
- Do not brag. If you are an accomplished player, let others discover how good you are.
- Profanity, vulgarities, and drinking will ruin your image. You may never recover your reputation.
- Don't be critical of other players, the club, the court, or the surroundings.
- Don't complain about being off your game that day.
- Don't make others wait unless you have an emergency. Talking on your cell phone is not usually an emergency.
- Don't play the victim when you lose or score badly. Don't blame something or someone.
- Don't argue about the score or someone's call.
- Don't be a loud mouth. Keep your voice at a reasonable pitch for the surroundings. In sports such as fishing and golf, remaining quiet is critical.
- Don't be a sponger. Bring your own balls and equipment. If you rent, have your gear fitted early and ready to use. You should remember that some players never lend their equipment to others. Bring extra balls.
- Don't blame or criticize if you lose the game because of your partner's poor showing.
- Don't boo or hiss at the other team or at the referee.
- Return any used equipment to the designated shelter—croquet balls and mallets, basketballs, or racquetball gear, for instance. Return everything in proper condition.
- Always shake hands, congratulate the winners, and thank the players for a good game.
- If you are a guest, you should always write a note of thanks to your host or hosts.

Private Clubs

When you are the guest at a private club, remember that though the rules may seem stuffy, they are supported and governed solely by the member. Here are some guidelines to observe when you are a guest at a private club:

- If you should arrive first, identify yourself to the doorman by giving your name and that of the member who invited you.
- Wait in the reception area or the room where you are escorted.
- Don't roam around even if the surroundings are lovely and you are curious; however, if the host offers, you may accept an invitation to tour the premises.
- Don't order food or beverage until your host arrives. Don't accept if it is offered until your host arrives.
- Don't ask about prices, which are usually not displayed.
- When the check comes, don't offer to pay, and don't comment when the host signs the check.
- Behave as though you are a guest in someone's home, respectful but at ease.
- Don't ask your host about membership, dues, or expenses, or compare one club to another.

Here are some tips to give you confidence when you are invited to a private club to play golf, tennis, or some other sport.

- Always carefully observe the rules. Obey all signs such as Do Not Enter, Members Only, or No Smoking.
- Ask your host about the proper attire at the club for a sporting event. If casual wear is appropriate, dress conservatively—no short shorts or bare midriffs for women or gaudy colored or patterned slacks for men.
- Don't tip anyone unless you ask your host about the club's policy.
- Your host will sign for food, beverages, and most or all of the services. You can repay your host later with a special outing.

Returning the Invitation

If you can reciprocate your host's invitation with one to your own club, do so on a later occasion. Don't apologize if your club does not appear equal in elegance or status. On the other hand, if you are invited to a club that does not measure up to yours in amenities, refusing the invitation is rude.

If you have no club membership, you can repay your host in another way. You may entertain him or her at a public course or at a nice restaurant.

Don't offer or attempt to repay in cash while you are still on the grounds of the club. If you are a close friend and are invited often, you may privately stick some bills into the member's pocket. Do this off the premises when no one can observe.

If your host is part of a corporate membership and the event is solely for the purpose of soliciting or keeping your business, you are not expected to pay back in kind; however, you should always write a thank-you note.

Most people prefer to pay their own way, but often you should graciously accept another's generosity and reciprocate the favor later. When you are invited to a private club, it is better to return the favor than offer cash unless your host invites you on a routine basis. However, if you are the only nonmember in a golf foursome, then cash is appropriate; but reimbursement must be made discreetly, according to the *National Etiquette Enterprises Newsletter.*[2]

Golf

Golf is increasingly becoming a main event in leisure and in business. There are camps you can go to learn the rudiments of the game, or you can ask a friend to teach you.

- If you are invited to a public course, pay your own greens fee, caddie fee, or cart fee. If the host refuses to allow you to pay, you must return the favor at a later date.
- If men and women tee off at the same distance, either may start first. The men's tee box is usually farther from the cup than the women's. In those circumstances the men tee off first.
- After the first hole the person with the lowest score on the previous hole tees off first.
- Players who are waiting must keep three things in mind: silence, stillness, and distance. You don't want to disturb the concentration of the player in progress. Even your shadow can be distracting.
- Slower players should allow others to play through.
- The player with the ball the greatest distance from the hole hits first.
- All the players should volunteer to help look for a lost ball. If you are the one with the lost ball, don't hold the game up for long.
- Players should not take too long to make a shot.
- Players should leave the field of play immediately after their turn.
- You should leave the area clean and in the same condition you found it. Don't litter.
- If you damage the surface of the green, you are expected to fix or replace the divot (a small piece of turf or earth dug up by a golf club in making too low a stroke).

- If your ball landed away from the green and in a sand trap or bunker, use the rake provided to cover your tracks and leave a smooth surface.
- If your ball is in the way, offer to replace it with a ball marker.
- You should offer to tend the pin (a stick with a numbered flag at the top that is placed in a hole to mark it).
- Never step on the imaginary line running between the player's ball and the cup.

Tennis

- Don't cross another court of players to get to your own. Don't retrieve your stray ball from such a court while their ball is in play.
- If a stray ball lands in your court, toss it back as soon as you can without interrupting your game.
- If the tennis net is sagging, secure it at the proper height before leaving.

Private clubs and public courses have specific guidelines and rules for their particular needs. You can learn them from the host member if you are a guest at a private club, or you can request a copy of them at public courses.

Remember that state and federal licenses and fees are applicable in sports such as hunting and fishing. Know and observe the laws governing the sport or activity in a particular state.

■■ ■■ ■■

A View of Manners from the Bible

Following the victorious army of Alexander the Great, the games and gymnastic sports of the Greeks were introduced into Palestine and a gymnasium was erected at Jerusalem. These athletic events delighted the Gentiles, but were repugnant to the pious Jews, because they were of a demoralizing character. Those who took part in these contests did so with naked bodies. Under the rule of the Maccabees, these spectacles came to an end; but Herod the Great revived them, building a theater at Jerusalem and similar ones in other places. The Romans carried on many of the Greek athletic customs but came to give special prominence to their gladiatorial shows.

When an athletic event was completed, the victor was presented with a palm branch by the judges. It was customary to give the winners a wreath made from the leaves of what was considered to be the sacred wild olive tree.[3]

Paul and the Incorruptible Crown

Paul refers to the incorruptible nature of the Christian's reward-crown in contrast to the perishable character of the prize in the Greek games.

Now everyone who competes exercises self-control in everything. However, they do it to receive a perishable crown, but we an imperishable one. Therefore I do not run like one who runs aimlessly, or box like one who beats the air. Instead, I discipline my body and bring it under strict control, so that after preaching to others, I myself will not be disqualified (1 Cor. 9:25–27).

Chapter 13

Dining in a Restaurant

Whether you are in a social or a business setting, your manners are nowhere more on display than at the dining table. And for many of us, few points of social etiquette are more worrisome. Even the most formal dinner should not intimidate you if you know and practice the basic rules and watch to see what the host or hostess does. Just as in a game, once you learn the rules and they become second nature, you will be able to dine in public with ease, enjoying the meal and the company.

One of life's most pleasant experiences is dining with others. Once you know what to expect and what is expected of you, you will know the right thing to do and be able to do it when the need arises. Good table manners come only from practice.

Business Dining in a Restaurant

Imagine that you have finally landed that second interview with a prestigious company, and someone in human resources is taking you out to dinner to discuss further the possibility of your going to work for the company. The rules for social etiquette apply more in a dining setting than in a corporate office, where everyone—whether male or female—defers to rank. For instance, men may help women with their chairs in a restaurant for business but not in a boardroom.

Learn the dress code for the particular restaurant as soon as the invitation is extended. You can call the place and ask, if necessary. Arrive at the restaurant a little early and wait for the host in the foyer area. Now is the time to turn off your cell phone or put it on vibrate.

When the host arrives, greet him or her with a smile and a firm handshake. Don't be shy, but follow the lead of the host, taking your cues from him or her in everything you do.

If there is a maitre d', hostess, or someone else to seat you, follow him or her to the table. Be seated where your host indicates or choose a chair after he or she does. Put your napkin in your lap when the host does, but don't touch anything else on the table such as your water or the crackers.

The two of you may chat a few minutes before ordering. It is the host's prerogative to bring up topics of business first. When it comes time to order, ask your host for suggestions or ask what he or she is ordering. That will give you an idea of the price range available to you. Don't order more courses than the host. In other words, if your host does not order an appetizer, skip that course yourself. Time may be short. If the host gives no indication as to what he or she is having, order something in the middle of the menu price range. Be sure to order something that is not messy to eat, such as spaghetti or ribs, no matter how much you like them. Never order an alcoholic beverage. Simply say, "I don't care for anything."

When the food arrives, watch your host carefully to see if your host says grace before eating. If a prayer is said, bow your head and remain absolutely quiet in this serious moment. If no grace is offered, pray silently.

Don't order condiments that are not on the table or not offered. To order catsup or steak sauce before tasting the food is regarded as inconsiderate. Say please and thank you often to the servers. Don't complain about the service, the atmosphere, the noise level, or anything else. Keep your focus on your host and the interview.

Never do any grooming at the table. Don't leave the table unless you must. If you do, excuse yourself, and go quietly to the rest room to blow your nose or put on lipstick. Don't spread papers out on the table when food is present as you might do in a business meeting.

If you discover something in your soup, discreetly tell your host that you need another bowl. He or she will summon the waiter and mention the problem. Unless something intolerable happens with your meal, don't make an issue of it; continue to discuss business and eat what you can, making no comments about bad food. It's not the host's fault, and eating is not your main purpose for being there. Pace the speed of your eating to match that of your host, if possible. No matter how tasty your entrée may be, do not ask for a doggy bag.

Don't monopolize the conversation, but listen carefully to the host, answering his or her questions as succinctly as possible. To prepare for good conversation, do your homework and know the names of the key people you may be working for and the primary purpose of the company and the department where you will be employed.

In this second interview the host may quiz you more on your personal likes and dislikes, such as hobbies or other interests. Be as open as possible without boring the host with the details of your latest motorbike race.

Write a thank-you note or letter later that day after the interview or as soon as possible.

Chapter 14

Dining in a Private Home

Dining rules are pretty much the same whether you are in a restaurant or in someone's home, but knowing the difference is important. Our mistakes and blunders become magnified when we are in a smaller, more intimate setting.

The key to successful dining in someone's home is to remember to follow the lead of the host or hostess. Don't touch anything until he or she does. That means your napkin, your water, or your silverware.

Compliment the cook on the food but not profusely. Don't ask for seconds unless they are offered. Then feel free to take more. If the food is served family style where each dish is passed around, take only your fair share of each dish. If there are four people at the table and there are four pork chops on the platter, take only one. Always think of the needs of your fellow diners, and you won't go wrong.

Here are some guidelines for in-home dining when you are the guest whether it's your date's house or someone else's.

One of the few times in life to be a little late is for a dinner party in someone's home, but be no more than ten minutes late. If you arrive early, you may inconvenience the hostess who is making last-minute preparations.

Never bring an uninvited guest unless you ask permission several days in advance of the dinner party. If you are the guest of honor, take or send a hostess gift. Flowers, as a hostess gift, should be delivered ahead of time, not taken with you as you go. The hostess will be too busy to put them in a vase. Any type of flower is appropriate in our country except red roses, which imply romance. The rule that the guest of honor must leave first is no longer viable.

All guests should stay thirty minutes to one hour after dinner unless they have informed the hostess beforehand that they must leave early.

The best time to do that is when she extends the invitation or as soon thereafter as possible.

Guests don't go into the kitchen before, during, or after the meal unless the hostess invites them. At family gatherings and informal get-togethers, your offer to help in cleaning up may be welcome. At formal dinners guests usually do not offer to help in the preparation or the cleanup. You will know if the dinner is a formal one by the attire, the service, and the formality of the table.

It is always the guests' responsibility to introduce themselves when appropriate. The host may be busy answering the door and attending other guests. If the host indicates partners before dinner, the men escort the women to the table. Husbands and wives do not sit together, but unmarried couples usually do. The reason for this rule is to facilitate the conversation around the table.

When dinner is ready, the host leads the way into the dining room with the female guest of honor, if there is one. The hostess and the male guest of honor, if there is one, go in last. A man assists the woman on his right with her chair, and also the woman on his left if she has no one to do it.

When being seated, a woman should assist in pulling her chair forward. To do that she grasps the sides of her chair and lifts it slightly as she and the man together move the chair forward and under the table. It may take more than one effort to reach a comfortable position.

If there are no place cards to indicate where you should sit, wait to be told. Never rearrange place cards. They are placed with thoughtful care according to protocol. Usually either the host or the hostess will ask guests to be seated. If you have no directions as to where to sit, you may take the chair nearest you when instructed to take a seat. The seating arrangement should be man, woman, man, woman when possible. After you are seated, don't touch anything, but watch the hostess.

The hostess will start with the invocation and then lift her napkin to place it in her lap. You should do the same. She will begin the actual dining process by picking up the proper piece of flatware, or she will tell her guests to begin.

If a piece of flatware or a glass is missing from your cover (place setting), quietly bring it to the hostess' attention by saying, "I seem to be missing a dinner fork."

Don't ask for seconds. If they are offered, you may accept, as long as others are still eating. Don't ask for condiments or special items not on the table. Taste everything before seasoning your food. It is considered an insult to the cook to season before tasting.

Don't ask what a dish is unless you compliment it first. Usually it is better not to ask questions about the food. Say thank you quietly each time you are served.

At the table, never mention allergies or ailments regarding food or drink. Simply eat what you can. If you do not like something, say, "I'm saving room for dessert." Do not wipe or scrape your plate clean. Diners are no longer required to leave food on the plate, but it is not rude to do so.

Always pick up your fork or spoon and at least pretend to eat each course. To see a tablemate not eating makes other guests feel uncomfortable and causes them to wonder if they should be eating the food set before them.

Use your napkin often, especially before sipping your beverage. Dab your mouth. Don't swipe side to side. Both men and women place the napkin in their lap with the folded edge toward their knees, while men drape the napkin over one leg. Women should not blot their lips on the napkin. Leave your napkin on your lap until the hostess places hers on the table, signaling that the meal is over.

Never leave a dinner table even temporarily unless it is absolutely necessary. If you must, place your napkin beside your place with the smudges hidden. Never put a napkin in a dirty plate. Never put used silverware back on the tablecloth. Prop the iced teaspoon on a plate or lay the bowl of it in another spoon to prevent staining the hostess's linens.

You may make complimentary statements about the food occasionally but not continuously.

Remember that your spouse or your date is a guest also. Treat him or her the same way you do other guests—without criticizing, arguing, or interrupting.

Be prepared to serve yourself from a platter or a large bowl if courses are presented to you by a server standing on your left. You may see two large serving pieces resting in the dish. The spoon goes in your right hand so that you can lift a serving portion from the serving dish and onto your plate. Place the spoon under a piece of meat, for instance, and secure it with the tines of the fork. To do so, hold the inverted fork in your left hand with your index finger on the spine and the handle pointing into the palm of your left hand.

If soup, sauce, or gravy is in the dish, suspend your portion above the container long enough for the drips to subside. Transfer it quickly to your plate. Don't plop your serving onto your plate. Slide the spoon gently from beneath your portion. Replace the serving utensils in the dish in such a way that they will not slide down into the dish. Usually, placing them in an inverted position helps by placing the bowl of the spoon and the tines of the fork facing downward.

Another formality served in a private home is afternoon tea. It is served from 3:00 to 5:00 P.M. High tea is a light meal much like our supper. It is served later than afternoon tea.

■■ ■■ ■■

A View of Manners from Bible Days

On ordinary occasions the people of the Bible period mostly sat or squatted on the floor around a low table at mealtime. The prophet Amos is the first biblical writer to refer to the custom of stretching themselves upon their couches when eating (Amos 6:4). By the time of Jesus, the Roman custom of reclining on couches at supper had been adopted in some Jewish circles. "There were three couches that were located on the three sides of a square, the fourth side being left open, so that a servant could get on the inside to assist in serving the meal." (Even today, we serve from the left). "The guest's position was to recline with the body's upper part resting on the left arm, and the head raised, and a cushion at the back, and the lower part of the body was stretched out."

Jesus said, "Many will come from east and west, and recline at the table with Abraham, Isaac, and Jacob in the kingdom of heaven" (Matt. 8:11).

The Sop at the Lord's Supper

We have to understand the customs of eating during Jesus' time to comprehend the meaning of His giving the sop to Judas. Some have thought that Judas was dipping into the dish at the same time as Jesus and that he was thus singled out as the betrayer. In truth, they were all dipping from the same large dish. Therefore, when Jesus said, "The one who dipped with Me in the bowl—he will betray Me" (Matt. 26:23), he was not identifying one. Jesus could have meant any one of them, but of course both Judas and Jesus knew who He meant.

The Sop

What is meant by the sop? It is the tastiest morsel of food being served at the feast. It may be served in a bread spoon but is more often picked up by the host with his thumb and finger and given to one of the guests as a sign of special friendship. Even today the sop is given to special honored guests in some parts of the world.

"The meaning of what Christ did then was most certainly to extend love and friendship to the very one who was going to betray Him. The act has been described as if the Lord were saying to the traitor:

"'Judas, my disciple, I have infinite pity for you. You have proved false, you have forsaken me in your heart; but I will not treat you as an enemy, for I have come not to destroy, but to fulfill. Here is my sop of friendship, and *that thou doest do quickly.*'"[1]

Chapter 15

General Table Manners for Any Occasion

- Place no elbows on the table unless all dishes are removed following the meal.
- Chew with your mouth closed.
- Hold the silverware correctly.

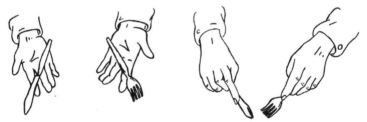

Hand Positions for Cutting

Used by permission from Dorothea Johnson, founder and director of The Protocol School of Washington®

- Cut one or two bites of meat at a time so your food won't get cold and your plate won't look messy.
- Pass food to the right. Place both the salt and pepper shakers on the table together for another diner to pick up. Set hot food on the table so your neighbor can pick it up by the handles. Pass the butter dish with the spreader on the dish.
- Servers should serve your food from the left and remove the soiled plate from the right. (Serving from the left prevents an accident with the diner who may be reaching for his or her beverage.)

- Beverages are served from the right.
- Break bread in half or pinch one bite at a time. Never take a big chomp out of food because your mouth will be wide open. No one wants to see your tonsils.
- Keep your feet flat on the floor and under the table, sitting up straight in your chair.
- Modify your voice so that only your tablemates can hear you.
- If you must leave the table, excuse yourself to the people on each side of you.
- Refuse food only if you must by saying, "No, thank you."
- Stir your iced tea quietly. Cover your hand to squeeze the lemon over the glass. You may drop the lemon in the glass, or if you don't care for lemon, remove it from the rim of the glass and place it on the dish beneath the glass or on your bread-and-butter plate. Put opened sweetener packets on the bread-and-butter plate.
- Say, "Please pass the . . ." when you need something. It should be passed to you by the shortest route. The rule about serving left to right applies to the first time around the table. After that, you should pass it the shortest way to the diner who needs it.
- Watch to see that all condiments near you are passed around the table.
- Unfold a dinner napkin halfway. Place the fold toward your knees. A small luncheon or paper napkin is opened completely.
- When the meal is finished, place your napkin, gently crumpled, to the left of your place setting. When excusing yourself momentarily, place your napkin beside your plate. (If you put it in your chair, you may get grease or food on the chair and then on your clothes when you return to your seat.)
- Eat at a moderate speed. Do not eat too fast or make others wait for you to finish.
- Place used silverware on a plate, not on the tablecloth.
- Eat quietly, making no noise with your mouth or silverware, if possible.
- Remove seeds, pits, gristles, etc. from your mouth with the utensil you used to put it in your mouth. Do not use your napkin because the discarded particle could get on your clothes or drop to the floor when you pick up your napkin later. Small bones may be removed with your thumb and forefinger for safety.
- Hold cold beverages by supporting the bowl of the glass from underneath, holding the bowl with your thumb and fingers on the stem.

- Refuse a beverage by simply saying, "No, thank you." No explanations are necessary. You can always drink water if only alcoholic drinks are served. Do not invert your cup or your glass to indicate that you are not drinking.

Chapter 16

Dining in a Restaurant with a Date or Other Guest

When a Man Hosts a Meal for a Female Guest

When a man is the host, he has more responsibilities than the guest(s). Perhaps you have finally asked that special someone out to eat and she has accepted. Now what to do? First, choose a restaurant you are familiar with and call for a reservation. Not all restaurants take reservations, but it's better to ask about them than to arrive with your date and have no table for the two of you.

When making the reservation, give your full name, phone number, the number of people in your group, your arrival time, and any special request such as recognition of your date's birthday. Some restaurants offer a piece of birthday cake with two forks, and the wait staff sings "Happy Birthday." If you plan to use a credit card, be sure to ask if the restaurant accepts your kind of card. You don't want to be embarrassed when it comes time to pay the check.

If you have to change your arrival time or find you will be a little late, be sure to call ahead so your table will not be given to someone else. It is also common courtesy to let the restaurant know if you have to cancel, so they can rebook the table.

When you and your date arrive at the restaurant, offer to let her out at the door, and go alone to park the car. She will wait just inside the restaurant door, and the two of you will enter the dining area together when you arrive. She may prefer to accompany you to the parking place.

If there is valet parking where an attendant parks your car and you tip him later, you both get out in front of the restaurant, leaving the keys in the ignition. The valet may open the car door for your date to exit before coming around to the driver's side. If not, she should wait for you to come around and open the door for her, as the valet slides behind the wheel.

Once the two of you are inside, you may or may not be asked to check your coats. Women usually take their coat with them to the table and drape it over the back of the chair with the lining exposed. However, it's convenient to check a wet raincoat, boots, umbrella, or packages. If you do check anything, you will need to leave a tip of $1.00 when you pick it up. If your date brought a handbag, she should place it in her lap. If it is too big, she may place it under her chair near her feet or in an empty chair at your table. It is not proper to place the bag on the table, to drape it over the back of the chair, or set it on the floor beside her for someone to stumble over.

If you as host see that a handbag could be a hazard in the walkway, you may suggest your date slide it under her chair.

When the headwaiter or hostess meets you at the entrance, give your name and mention that you have a reservation. Your date then follows the headwaiter to the table, and you walk behind her. If the table reserved for you is unacceptable because it is just outside the kitchen doorway, you may ask for a better one.

At a regular table the waiter may hold the chair for your date while you wait until she is settled comfortably before taking your seat. If you are directed to a banquette, wait for the waiter to pull out the table and allow your date to slide in first. If the restaurant expects patrons to seat themselves, you lead the way to a table and pull out a chair for your date.

Ordering

You as the host should suggest something to your date to alert her to your budget for the evening, or you can simply say, "Order anything you like." Today it is still proper for the man to order for the lady, but often the waiter will look directly at the lady and ask for her choice. If that occurs, she should speak up and give him her order. If you or your date want your food prepared in a certain way, request it when you order. If you are unable to read the menu or need an explanation about a specific type of food, don't be afraid to ask the waiter. Trying new food can be fun. You may even ask the waiter to show you how to eat escargot, crab legs, lobster, or any food you have not eaten before.

If you are permitted to order for your date, usually you will give only the entrée item to the waiter, and then he will ask her how she wants it cooked and what kind of salad dressing she wants. It is not proper for her to relay her choices through you to the waiter who is standing there waiting to hear it.

Cutting Bread

When a loaf of bread is placed on the table, the host should slice off two or three portions, take one, and offer the remainder to the people beside him. Then pass the whole loaf on the board or in a breadbasket around the table for each man to cut off a portion for himself and the woman next to him. She retrieves the piece and passes the board or basket to the right.

The Maid in the Ladies' Room

If a man's date needs to do more than apply some lipstick, she should excuse herself to the rest room while he takes care of the check. On a date but not in business, a woman may apply lipstick without a mirror at the table, but no other grooming is proper. A businesswoman excuses herself even to apply lipstick.

When a man's date leaves for the rest room, she may find an attendant there with a clean towel or hand lotion. It is customary to leave a small tip (fifty cents to one dollar) in a dish placed in open view. If it's a posh restaurant, the man should make sure his date has change before she goes to the rest room.

On a Double Date

When two couples go out together to eat, the ladies usually sit opposite each other. However, if one couple is hosting the other (or a group of people), the host and hostess sit facing each other in order to care for their guests.

Calling the Elusive Waiter

Sometimes it seems that the waiter has left the premises. You need service—a refill on tea or a fork for your dessert. It is never proper to whistle or snap your fingers, but you can try one of the following: Stare at the waiter, hoping he will look your way. When he does, you may raise one hand with a slight beckoning motion. If he is close enough to speak to him without shouting, simply say, "Waiter," when he looks your way. Or if the headwaiter, another waiter, or even the busboy goes by your table, you may ask him to call your waiter for you. It is permissible to call a female waitress *miss*, "but *sir* is not correct for a waiter, whether used by a woman, man, or youngster," according to *Emily Post's Etiquette*.[1] *Server* is the word most often used today.

If your date has to leave the table for some reason, you should stand and help her with her chair, if necessary. She simply excuses herself quietly and leaves the napkin in loose folds beside her plate with any smudges hidden from view.

The same general table manners apply whether you are in a home or a restaurant (see pages 98–100).

When the two of you have finished your meal and are ready to leave, you will ask for the check and go over the figures mentally to check for accuracy. If there is a mistake, quietly mention it to the waiter who will take the check back to the cashier for correction.

Paying the Check

There are several ways that restaurants collect for the check. If the waiter takes your money and returns with the change, pick it up and leave the tip. Fifteen percent of the bill is still the accepted tip everywhere except in fancy restaurants where 20 percent is expected. The tip is usually divided up by the manager among the wait staff who attended your table. If the service was extremely poor, you may leave a small tip or none at all; but if you do so, you should quietly tell the manager or headwaiter about the problem, remembering not to blame bad food on the waiter. Also, take into account how many tables the waiter had to service. Sometimes waiters have to do double duty.

If you are using a credit card, the waiter will fill in the subtotal and leave space for you to add the tip, total the bill, and sign the credit slip. The waiter will give you one copy and keep the rest.

If the check says, "Please pay the cashier," you will leave the correct amount for the tip on the table and stop at the cashier to pay the check on your way out. If you do not have correct change for the tip, simply return to the table after paying the check and leave the tip then.

When it is time to leave the table, it is courteous for the male to help his date get up from her chair and put on her coat, making sure that neither of you leaves anything behind. Your date exits the restaurant first with you opening doors for her and following behind. If you checked anything at the entrance, simply deposit fifty cents or one dollar in the plate at the checkroom. It's always a good idea to carry a small roll of one-dollar bills for tips.

Outside the restaurant, you will give the card or slip of paper that identifies your car to the valet attendant and wait for him to bring it around. You or the attendant may open the car door for your date. Before leaving, remember to tip the attendant for his services. The appropriate amount is two dollars unless you are in an expensive, upscale restaurant or hotel; then the tip should be three dollars.

On leaving the restaurant, it is nice for the lady to say something complimentary about the evening—the food, the choice of restaurant, or some other pleasantry.

When a Woman Hosts a Meal with a Male Guest

A woman has these responsibilities when she invites a man to dine with her:

- She asks him to be her guest so he will know what his role is to be.
- She makes the reservations ahead of time.
- She suggests something for him to have on the menu so he will feel comfortable about the price of his choice.
- She asks the waiter to bring the check to her unless she has arranged beforehand to give the restaurant her credit card number, in which case she and her guest may simply leave the table when they finish.

Chapter 17

Special Situations

It is permissible to order different dishes and sample your partner's food if it is done unobtrusively. For instance, if your date wants to try your coq au vin (chicken cooked in wine), you can pass your plate to her to get a small portion of chicken with her fork. She should not reach over and spear it herself, nor should you use your fork to give her a taste. This way food is not strewn across the table.

If the man gets his food or his date gets hers and it is not cooked the way requested, it is the man's responsibility to get the attention of the waiter to tell him/her quietly, but specifically, what should be done to the food. If a glass is not clean or a clean utensil is needed, follow the same procedure. The date stays out of the discussion.

If you pass the table of a group of friends unexpectedly on the way in or on the way out, simply say hello and move on. If you should need to stop for a moment, the men at the table rise for women, and you quickly introduce your date if there are no more than four or five people. Be sure not to linger, crowding the aisle and letting the diners' food get cold while you chat.

Tipping the Headwaiter

Tipping the headwaiter is necessary only if he or she has gone to extra trouble to accommodate you, such as moving tables together for your group or party or taken special care of getting your steak cooked properly. Upon leaving, simply give five dollars or more to the headwaiter in a handshake.

Going Dutch

The term "going Dutch" means that everyone pays for his own meal. The wording of the invitation is the key to knowing whether the outing will be Dutch treat or one person will be paying for everyone. "Let's meet after work for a pizza" is not necessarily an offer to pay. "I'd like to take you out to lunch" usually means the inviter expects to pay. In situations where friends go Dutch, there are several ways to pay the check. Each person orders his or her own meal and gets a separate check. Otherwise, one person can collect enough money from everyone to cover the check and the tip. Or one person can use his or her own money or credit card, and members of the group pay back outside the restaurant.

The admonition here is to avoid that ridiculous situation where each diner tries to add up exactly his or her share and argues about whose dinner cost more. Any discussions should take place outside the restaurant.

Chapter 18

Formal Dining

The most formal meal is the dinner with at least five courses: soup, fish, sorbet, a main dish (entrée) of meat or fowl, salad, dessert, and coffee. The courses may or may not be in that order.

The host will tell you where to sit, or you will look for your name on a place card. Wait until everyone is around the table and ready to sit down before doing so. A man seats the lady on his right.

Once you are seated, you may see more silverware and glasses than you ever thought existed. Don't be nervous. Usually, the tableware is set for practical use. That is, it is arranged in the order in which you will use it.

Silverware

The first pieces of flatware to be used should be in logical sequence. Work from the outside moving inward toward the plate as you progress through the meal. Flatware is arranged in the proper order for you to use it.

If your place setting is improperly set, it should be obvious to you. Use common sense. If soup is the first course served and the outside pieces are a knife and fork, you will look for the large, rounded spoon used for sipping soup. Any time you are unsure which piece to use, watch your hostess. She will choose the correct one.

Sometimes the servers will bring the necessary dining pieces when they bring the dish containing the next course. For instance, sorbet,

In China, children are allowed to use spoons for everything until they are about three or four years old, when chopstick training begins.[1]

—Margaret Visser, *The Rituals of Dinner*

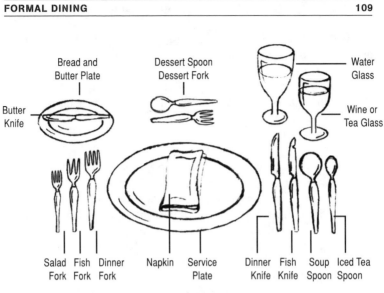

Bread and Butter Plate — Dessert Spoon Dessert Fork — Water Glass

Butter Knife — Wine or Tea Glass

Salad Fork · Fish Fork · Dinner Fork — Napkin — Service Plate — Dinner Knife · Fish Knife · Soup Spoon · Iced Tea Spoon

Formal Dining

served just before the entrée, usually comes with a small spoon on a side plate.

Knives and spoons will be on your right with the forks on the left. The seafood fork is the only fork you will find on the right side of your plate. It will be on the extreme right or it will come with the seafood (usually as an appetizer).

The dessert fork and spoon will be above your dinner plate, or you may find them along either side of the plate and adjacent to it. Sometimes they are brought with your dessert.

> *English words* soup *and* supper *come from* sop, *the soaked bread that so often used to fill out the broth in its bowl.*[2]
>
> —Margaret Visser, *The Rituals of Dinner*

If after careful observation, you pick up the wrong utensil, simply go on eating with it and ask the waiter or the hostess for another one before the next course.

Glasses and Cups

Glasses and cups are always on your right, even if you are left-handed. Glasses arranged in the order they are to be used are placed above the knife and soup spoon. The water glass should be placed above the tip of the knife. This beverage is nearest the center at the top of your plate. The iced tea glass is on the right of the water goblet.

Use the other glasses in the order they are placed. Begin with the glass farthest to your right. Each glass is removed as you finish the course assigned to it. Occasionally, the server will bring the glass when he or she brings the beverage.

The Plates

The only plates you may see are a bread-and-butter plate (top left) and the service plate (also called a charger) directly in front of you. Service plates are quite large. Your courses will be brought in individual dishes and placed on this plate. Your service plate will be removed immediately before your dinner plate (entrée) is brought.

The bread-and-butter plate should be on the left above your forks. It is a good depository for paper wrappings and even for small finger foods. The bread-and-butter knife is smaller than the dinner knife. If you have one, it will rest across the top of the bread-and-butter plate.

In truly formal meals, the salad is served as a course; however, at banquets we often see the salad plate on the table when we sit down. If so, the salad fork will be to the left of the forks.

The Napkin

Usually, you will see the napkin folded decoratively and placed in the center of your service plate. Other places for it are to the left of the forks or beneath the forks if space is limited.

In a restaurant the napkin is lifted and placed in your lap as soon as everyone is seated. In many upscale restaurants, the maitre d' will drape the napkin in each diner's lap. In a home the hostess signals the time to begin by placing her napkin in her lap.

Both men and women leave a large dinner napkin folded in half as they place it on their lap. Men drape a napkin over one leg and place the folded edge of the large napkin toward the cuff of their trousers. Similarly, women drape the napkin across their lap with the folded edge toward the hem of their skirt. Small luncheon napkins are opened fully onto your lap or leg.

The reason behind placing the fold toward the knees is interesting. If you pick up the napkin by its folded edge, dab your mouth, and replace it with the fold pointed toward your cuffs or hem, you will not get grease or a food stain on your clothes.

To use the napkin once your food arrives, reach toward your knees and lift the napkin by its folded edge. After dabbing the corners of your mouth with it, replace the napkin in your lap. Any smudge or stain will then be exposed on the napkin and in a way that won't soil your dress or trousers.

The napkin remains in your lap until you get up to leave the restaurant. If you must leave the table for any reason during the meal, simply place the napkin loosely to the left of your plate. Retrieve it when you return. Some etiquette teachers say to drop the napkin in your chair when you leave the table temporarily, but you will risk getting food or grease on the chair seat and then on your clothing.

The Blessing

In someone's home the blessing is often said before the hostess picks up her napkin. In a restaurant the blessing is usually said after the food arrives.

Serving the Meal

The rules for serving have remained traditionally the same since the late 1800s. Instructions for dining are always given for the right-handed person. If you are left-handed, simply reverse the instruction when necessary, but don't rearrange the place setting. For both left-handed and right-handed individuals, food is served from their left, and each course is removed from their right. To help you remember, think of the letters *L* and *R:* lower from the left; remove from the right.

Beverages are poured and glasses cleared from the right. Nothing except your lips should ever touch the rim of a glass.

If the sugar or artificial sweeteners are within your reach in front of you, pick up the container, take what you need, and pass the container to your right. You may wish to offer it to the person sitting on your left next to you before taking one for yourself. Once you begin the container's passage around a large table, you may never see it again to serve yourself.

Everyone at the table should do the same with any condiments he sees in front of him. If you need the salad dressing, for instance, and no one passes it around, simply say, "Please pass the salad dressing." Then the container should be passed to you by the shortest route, regardless of the direction.

Preparing the Beverages

To prepare a beverage with sugar or an artificial sweetener, tear open the package and empty the contents into the glass or cup. Gently fold the paper and place it on your bread-and-butter plate or on the plate beneath the glass or cup.

If you use lemon, cover the wedge with your left hand and squeeze it with your right hand. You may choose to drop the lemon wedge into the glass or cup and press it with the iced teaspoon to release the juice, being careful not to make noise. The iced teaspoon is the one with the longest handle.

Place the spoon on the underlying plate. If there is no plate under the iced tea glass, invert the bowl of the spoon and prop it on another plate with the tip of the handle resting on the table. The iced teaspoon is the only utensil you will ever prop. Or, you may place the wet bowl of the teaspoon on another piece of flatware or on your empty sugar packet. If you replace the used spoon on the table, the tea will permanently stain the cloth.

The courses in formal dinners do not necessarily come in the same order; however, the sorbet must be served immediately before the entrée to cleanse the palate.

American and Continental Style of Dining

From this point onward, the diner will eat using either American style or the Continental (also called European) style of dining. Both styles are acceptable, but it is not proper to switch back and forth during a course. As Americans, we are the only diners in the world who shift our knife and fork from hand to hand while eating. For that reason it is called American style.

From caveman days people have put food in their mouths with their right hand. It was not until a few short centuries ago that Europeans began to eat with what we now call the Continental style—inverted fork in the left hand and knife in the right hand. The upper class changed to the Continental style to make a class distinction between the rich and the poor. Soon all classes of people ate that way. That was when etiquette was considered snobbish. Today it is simply thoughtful behavior. Americans continue to eat the original way.[3]

—Margaret Visser, *The Rituals of Dining*

The American Style

For right-handed people the fork is held in the left hand and the knife in the right hand. After cutting a bite of food, put the knife down with the cutting edge toward you and exchange the fork from the left hand to the right. The right-handed American diner holds the fork in the right hand and gently spears the morsel before placing it in the mouth.

The Continental Style

Today the Continental style is used by the rest of the world and by many Americans. The fork is held in the left hand with the tines down. The index finger is placed on the spine of the fork. The knife is held in the right hand with the index finger on the dull side of the blade. The rounded tip of the knife handle pushes into the palm of the right hand.

The knife is used to cut food and to help push food onto the back of the fork. There is no shifting of utensils. The diner continues to hold the knife in the right hand while placing the fork, tines down and laden with food, into the mouth.

It is proper to choose either American style eating or Continental, but it is not proper to eat your meat, for instance, with the left hand and the fork tines turned down and then to switch the fork to the right hand to eat your vegetables. You must choose one style or the other for the complete meal. Yes, that means if you choose Continental style, you must eat your peas on the back of your fork that is held in your left hand—no easy feat.

> *I eat my peas with honey—*
> *I've done it all my life.*
> *It makes the peas taste funny*
> *But it keeps them on my knife.*

Correct Continental

Correct American

Incorrect Cutting

Correct Cutting

A Formal Meal

The following is an example of a formally served meal. The order in which courses are served may vary from culture to culture, but the sorbet must always be served immediately prior to the entrée.

The Soup Course

Hold the soup spoon with the handle between your index finger and the middle finger. Your thumb will rest on top. Dip the soup away from you with the spoon in a horizontal position.

Move the bottom of the spoon across the back of the soup bowl to remove any excess soup that might drip. For cream soup, sip from the side of the spoon without making noise. For chunky soup, you will use your teeth to gently retrieve the chunk from the spoon.

If there are handles on the bowl, you may tip the bowl away from you to get the last of the soup with the spoon. When resting, sipping your beverage, or using your napkin, place the spoon on the little plate beneath the bowl—never in the bowl. This will prevent an accident with a protruding spoon handle.

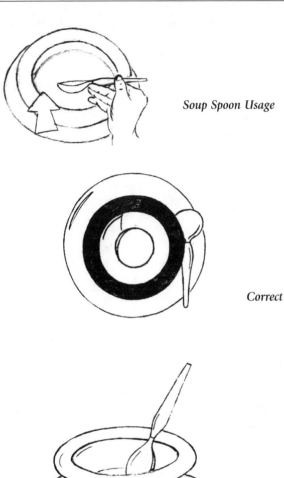

Soup Spoon Usage

Correct

Incorrect

The soup is sometimes presented in a shallow soup plate with side rims. You may then place the spoon horizontally in the bowl with no fear of a mishap. It is difficult to place the spoon between the rim of a soup plate and the service plate beneath it.

The Salad Course

When the lettuce is properly prepared in the kitchen, you don't need a knife. You can leave it on the table while you eat the salad with only a salad fork. Using a knife to cut lettuce was once forbidden because the vinegar in the salad dressing would tarnish the knife blade. That was before stainless steel.

Unfortunately, you sometimes face what looks like a whole head of lettuce. A knife is essential. In a properly set formal setting, you'll find a salad knife on your right; but often this is not available, and you are forced to use the only knife, the dinner knife.

When you must use the dinner knife for anything before the entrée, rest it on the bread-and-butter plate when you finish the salad; otherwise, the knife will disappear when the salad is removed or later with the service plate. Do not place used silverware back on the tablecloth.

If you lose your dinner knife, ask a server to bring you another. If the salad is served with cheese, use your knife to place a small portion on your salad plate. Then use a knife to spread cheese on one cracker or piece of bread at a time.

When you finish eating the salad course, place the salad fork and salad knife (if you have one) in the "finished position" (see illustration on page 118) even if you used only the fork.

The Fish Course

In a formal meal the fish course may be one of many courses or the main dish. It is usually baked or grilled and served either in portions or as a whole fish. The Continental style works best for eating fish.

The fish knife and fork are easy to recognize. The placement on the table of the fish fork on the left will correspond with that of the fish knife on the right. The knife has a wide, dull blade with a notch on the top.

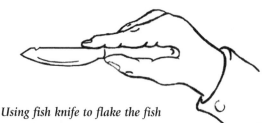

Using fish knife to flake the fish

Fish Served in Portions

To eat fish served in portions, hold the fish fork in your left hand, tines down. Hold the fish knife by steadying the knife in your right hand between your pointed index finger and curved middle finger. The knife handle should rest on the web between your thumb and index finger.

Use the fish knife to flake the fish and guide it onto the back of your fork tines. Fish is tender; therefore, it should be flaked, not cut as you would a piece of meat.

If you choose to eat only in the American style, you may use the fish fork alone. Leave the knife on the table and hold the fork in your right hand with the tines up. When you finish eating the fish, place both the knife and fork in the 10:20 position, as taught by Dorothea Johnson, founder and director of The Protocol School of Washington®. Each handle will extend about an inch over the rim of the plate. Never gangplank (or prop) the fork and knife with the ends of the handles resting on the table like oars in a boat.

Fish Served Whole

The notch on the fish knife is used to separate the halves of a whole fish. When fish is served whole, use the notch to separate the top and bottom halves.

As you eat the fish, remove any small bones from your mouth with your thumb and index finger. Place them on the side of your plate or on the plate provided for the bones. When you finish eating the fish course, place the fork and knife in the "finished" position (see illustration on page 118). The only time you may put your fingers in your mouth is to retrieve a bone.

After eating the top filet, slip the knife between the other filet and the backbone. Lift away the backbone and place it on the side of your plate or on the plate provided for bones. Then you may eat the remainder of the fish.

Fork and Knife gangplanked

The Finished Position for the Flatware

The Protocol School of Washington teaches students to imagine that a plate is the face of a clock. For the finished position the diner should place the knife in the 10:20 position with the cutting edge of the knife facing the center of the plate. The tip of the knife should point to 10:00 and the handle to 4:00.

Place the fork, tines down, parallel to and just below the knife. The tips of the handles will extend about an inch over the lower right side of the plate.

American Style

The "resting" position for the American style is simply to lay the fork on your plate as you are holding it, not in the 10:20 position. The resting position shows that the diner has not finished eating that course.

Finished Position

Resting Continental

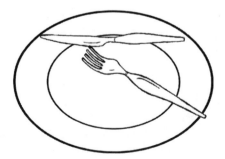

Resting American

Unfortunately, not all restaurant servers know about the signal. If a waiter attempts to remove your plate, simply say, "I have not finished."

The Sorbet Course

Sorbet is frozen fruit juice and contains no milk solids. It is a palate cleanser served in a compote or dish on an underlying plate. It is always served immediately before the entrée. A spoon usually accompanies the course when it is served.

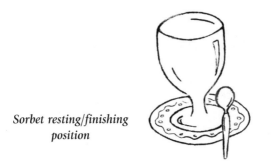

Sorbet resting/finishing position

A small spoon will be on the underlying plate when the server brings this course. Leave the spoon on the plate when you are resting and when you finish. You may use your left hand to steady the compote or dish.

Eat the sorbet as you would soup, by removing any drips from the spoon when you move it across the back rim of the compote. However, since sorbet has a small spoon, you may put it in your mouth, rather than sip from the side as you do when eating soup. The garnish may be eaten but is usually left on the underlying plate.

The Entrée (Main Course)

A dinner knife must be held properly for cutting meat or fowl. For both American and Continental style, the method of cutting meat or fowl is the same. The end of the knife handle should point into your right palm. Press down firmly with the index finger that rests on the dull edge of the knife blade and points toward the tip.

Hold the fork in your left hand with the tines down. Rest your index finger on the spine of the inverted fork. Pierce and secure the meat with the fork. Place the cutting edge of the knife slightly in front of the tines of the fork. Pull the knife blade toward you to cut the meat. Cut only one or two bites at a time.

A small wedge of vegetable may be speared onto the tines of the fork along with the meat. Be careful not to stack food on the fork.

The Difficult-to-Eat Dessert

Have you ever tried to eat food that went skidding off the plate when you put your fork or spoon to it? Frozen desserts often do that.

To avoid such a disaster, pick up the dessert fork and spoon that are above your plate or along either side of your plate. Hold the fork in your left hand, tines down.

Eat with the spoon and use the inverted fork held in your left hand to secure a difficult dessert, such as a frozen one, while you spoon into it.

When you finish eating, place the fork and spoon in the "finished" position even if you used only one of them. When the meal is complete, your place should be clear of all silverware, except possibly a coffee spoon if coffee will be served at the table.

Other Desserts

Eat pie or cake with only the dessert fork. Eat ice cream or pudding with the dessert spoon. If you use only one utensil, leave the other one on the table while you eat. Then place both the fork and spoon on the plate when you finish.

Toasting Protocol

The host may make a toast before the appetizer or right before dessert. While remaining seated, he or she may make a toast before the meal to greet everyone. In anticipation of a toast, guests refrain from touching any of the beverages before the meal begins.

The British upper class began the habit of putting buttered toast, often with sugar and nutmeg in the butter, in a glass of wine to make it special. Raising your glass to someone was called "toasting." The glass was passed around and the last one to receive it got the buttered toast.[4]

—Margaret Visser, *The Rituals of Dinner*

At the beginning of the dessert course, a host may propose a toast to honor one individual. For this closing gesture the host stands. The honored guest remains seated. The guest may hold a glass but should not drink to toast himself. Afterward the honored person may then rise and propose a toast in which he or she may participate. After the honored guest finishes, another guest may rise to propose a toast.

When a toast is proposed, it is acceptable to sip water from your water goblet, or simply to raise any beverage glass you have.

"President George W. Bush gave up alcohol 16 years ago. He uses water for toasts at state occasions."[5]

"Toasting was used during the eighteenth century to force guests to learn one another's names. When toasting began they would have to drink to healths, calling out their companions' names."[6]

—Margaret Visser, *The Rituals of Dinner*

The Meal Is Completed

The host signals that it is time to leave the table by placing his or her napkin to the left of the place setting. The plates may or may not have been removed. The napkin will rest loosely on the table with any unsightly smudges on the underside.

The guests then do the same with their napkins. Never refold a napkin. Never put a napkin in a used plate or glass.

Practice Makes Perfect

To acquire skill and confidence, you must practice your fine dining skills. Don't be frazzled at the sight of many forks or frightened by formalities.

Use as many of the new skills as possible every time you eat, wherever you are. Then you won't be overwhelmed and frustrated by details when you need to use the finer points of formal dining.

If you make a mistake or forget a rule, don't be discouraged. Relax and follow the lead of the host or that of others if no host is present. If you do everything slowly and carefully, you will look confident and avoid any embarrassing mishaps. Then when you get home, look up the rule. You will probably never forget that one again.

Chapter 19

Buffets and Other Forms of Stand-up Eating

- Be attentive to your host for instructions to bow your head for the invocation or when to begin.
- Wait to be told before approaching the food that is displayed. At the same time, remember that someone has to go first and the hostess is waiting.
- Look for the napkins and plates. Begin your trip around the table there. Place your napkin under your plate.
- Position a cup of punch or other beverage on your plate when you are handed one, before you finish filling your plate. Beverages are typically placed at the end of the line.
- Never appear to be eating from the buffet table, snack table, or serving dish. First, transfer the food to your buffet plate or hold a napkin under the item while you retreat from the food area to eat it.
- Never take a bite from a morsel and then return it to the container or the table.
- Never fish around for a submerged chip or vegetable using your fingers.
- Generally, hot food is eaten with a fork or spoon and cold food is eaten with a toothpick or sometimes with your fingers.
- Never put soiled toothpicks used in hors d'oeuvres back into the dish or on the buffet table. Collect used ones on the side of your plate or in your paper napkin until you find a wastebasket or receptacle provided for such things.
- Don't heap your plate or stuff your mouth.

- Don't ever spit anything out of your mouth. If you have a paper napkin, you may remove the offending tidbit with that.

- Don't put your own utensil into any communal dish. For instance, don't put your fork in the relish dish, and don't put a wet spoon in the sugar bowl.

- Choose only one or two pieces of food from a main dish (such as meat) unless directed otherwise or unless there is a variety.

- Don't place wet glasses or dishes on the furniture. Ask for a coaster or use a napkin.

- Do not leave a soiled plate and glass for other guests to look at after you finish. Take your things to a place usually provided for used dinnerware.

- Do apologize and offer to assist in the clean up if you make a mess.

Chapter 20

Rules for Joining a Club

You may be invited to go through what is called rush week, in which a private club, sorority, fraternity, or other organization may choose certain individuals and reject others to become members. Here are some guidelines to follow as you participate in such a selection process. Your reaction to the results of whether you are chosen is more important than the selection process itself. Approach it as just another experience.

Rush week is a two-way street. You should be looking for the right group for you, just as the organization is looking for appropriate new members to join them.

Guidelines

- Develop the right attitude. Some groups cut prospects each evening for many different reasons. Don't worry about why you were cut.
- Schedule enough time to dress for each party, giving special attention to grooming and accessories. Less makeup and fewer accessories are preferred for women.
- Enter a room with a confident smile, not a cocky attitude.
- Don't cling to one friend. Be outgoing and friendly.
- When talking to a member, ask questions and be expressive. Your credentials, such as grade average and accomplishments, are already on record.
- Say such things as, "This group seems to do so much. What is the most popular project?" Every organization is looking for talented people. You may talk about projects you have worked on but don't brag.
- Listen more than you talk. Respond with enthusiasm in a way

the talker will know you really listened. Try to use each member's name.

- Don't talk about all your friends back home. Be interested in the present. For instance, say you are looking forward to learning about that organization and all other college activities.
- Be prepared to ask questions. Don't say, "I don't have any."
- Don't be silly, loud, or too serious. Laugh at their skits and laugh at yourself when the opportunity arises.
- Don't appear too eager. Don't drop hints about being invited to join another group.
- Don't say, "I'll just die if I don't get invited to join this group."
- If you are concerned about policies, expenses, or time requirements, now is the time to ask. Evaluate your situation. Don't just go along with the group.
- If you don't get a bid to join this group, remember there are other organizations. Get involved and keep a good attitude.
- Whichever group you join, get the name of the alumni president from your hometown and write a thank-you note to the entire alumni.[1]

■■ ■■ ■■

A View of Manners from Bible Days

It's the nature of the common man to want to be part of a group whether it's a club, a team, or an association. In some groups members are chosen to join while others are rejected. But no one likes a pushy, aggressive, dominator to be among those contending for choice positions.

The following Scripture passage clearly gives Jesus' message regarding how we should act. Mark 10:35–45:

Then James and John, the sons of Zebedee,
approached Him and said, "Teacher, we want You to do
something for us if we ask You."

"What do you want Me to do for you?" He asked
them.

"Grant us," they answered Him, "that we may sit at
Your right and at Your left in Your glory."

But Jesus said to them, "You don't know what you're
asking. Are you able to drink the cup I drink, or to be
baptized with the baptism I am baptized with?"

"We are able," they told Him.

But Jesus said to them, "You will drink the cup

I drink, and you will be baptized with the baptism I am baptized with. But to sit at My right or left is not Mine to give, but it is for those for whom it has been prepared." When the other ten disciples heard this, they began to be indignant with James and John.

And Jesus called them over and said to them, "You know that those who are regarded as rulers of the Gentiles dominate them, and their men of high positions exercise power over them. But it must not be like that among you. On the contrary, whoever wants to become great among you must be your servant, and whoever wants to be the first among you must be a slave to all. For even the Son of Man did not come to be served, but to serve, and to give His life—a ransom for many."

Chapter 21

Patriotism

Since the tragedy of September 11, 2001, there has been a renewed spirit of patriotism among the citizens of our country. The flag is a proud symbol of our nation and should be respected at all times.

When a national flag is raised or lowered in a ceremony or when it passes by in a parade or in a review, everyone should stand to attention and face it. You should rise for a pledge to another country's flag, but you should not pledge allegiance to that country.

Women should stand quietly with their hands at their sides, or they may place their right hands over their hearts. Men remove their hats and hold them over their hearts in their right hands. Only military personnel render the military salute as the flag passes. A man without a hat salutes by placing his right hand over his heart.

When the Pledge of Allegiance to the flag is spoken at a public dinner or in church, men and women stand quietly at attention (with their hands hanging loosely at their sides) while repeating it or listening to the person saying the pledge.

Everyone remains standing until the flag(s) have been carried out of view before being seated.

The National Anthem

Everyone, children and adults, should stand for the playing of "The Star Spangled Banner." If you are on your way to your seat, or in any public place, when you hear the first few bars of the song, you should stop where you are, face toward the music, and stand at attention until it is finished. When the National Anthem is played and the flag is not displayed, only those in military uniform should salute at the first note of the anthem. Do not talk, chew gum, eat, or drink during the song.

When you are at home or alone and you hear the anthem played on the radio or television, it is not necessary to stand. However, if the orchestra at a large party plays the anthem, the guests do rise and stand at attention, facing the music.

Flag Etiquette

The following is part of the Federal Flag Code as distributed by Veterans of Foreign Wars of the United States, VFW Building, 406 West 34th Street, Kansas City, Missouri 64111:

In 1942, Congress passed a joint resolution adopting an official Flag Code stating the procedures for properly handling and displaying the flag.

- The flag should be hoisted briskly and lowered ceremoniously.
- The flag is never allowed to touch the ground or the floor.
- When hung over a sidewalk on a rope extending from a building to a pole, the union stars are always away from the building.
- When vertically hung over the center of the street, the flag always has the union stars to the north in an east-west street, and to the east in a north-south street.
- The flag of the United States of America should be at the center and at the highest point of the group when a number of flags of states or localities or pennants of societies are grouped and displayed from staffs.
- The flag should never be festooned, drawn back, or up in folds but always allowed to fall free.
- The flag should be displayed at half-staff until noon on Memorial Day then raised to the top of the staff.
- Never fly the flag upside down except as a signal of distress in instances of extreme danger to life or property.
- The flag is never flown in inclement weather except when using an all-weather flag.
- The flag can be flown every day from sunrise to sunset and at night if illuminated properly.

The code also states that a worn or soiled flag should be properly disposed of by fire.

Food Glossary

Many menus in upscale restaurants are filled with French and Italian words because the French and Italians are considered among the finest cooks in the world. Here is a list of terms (with the pronunciation) that you will see in many upscale restaurants.

Agneau	ah-nyoh′	lamb
à la carte	ah lah cart	each item priced separately
à la mode	ah lah mode	with ice cream
antipasto	an tih pas toh	Italian appetizer
au gratin	oh grah-tan	with cheese
au jus	oh zhoo	with gravy
au lait	oh leh	with milk
béarnaise	ba–ar-neze	a sauce
beurre	buhr	butter
bifteck	beef-teck	beef steak
boeuf	buhf	beef
bisque	bisk	cream soup
bouillabaisse	bou-ee-va-bess	fish stew or soup
bouillon	boo-yon	clear broth
brie	bree	semisoft cheese
café	ka-fay	coffee
café au lait	ka-fay oh leh	coffee with milk
café noir	ka-fay nwahr	black coffee
canard	ka-nar	duck
champignons	shahm-pee-nyon	mushrooms
crème	krem	cream
crêpes	krep	pancakes

crevette	kruh-veht′	shrimp
côte	koht	chop
côtelette	ko′telet	lamb chop
côtelette de porc	ko′telet duh pork	pork chop
croissant	krwa-san	crescent-shaped pastry
déjeuner	day-ju-nay	lunch
demitasse	dem-ee-tas	small cup of coffee
en croûte	ahn kroot	baked in a crust
entrée	ohn-tray	main course
escargots	ess-car-go	snails
filet mignon	fi-lay meen yon	boneless beef tenderloin
flambé	flahm-bay	flamed
florentine	flor-en-teen	with spinach
foie gras	flwah-grah	goose liver
fromage	fro-mazh	cheese
gâteau	ga-toe	cake
glace	glahs	ice cream
haricots verts	ah-ree-ko vehr	green beans
homard	o-mar	lobster
hors d′oeuvres	or-durv	appetizers
maitre d′hotel (maitre d′)	meh-tra dotell	headwaiter
mousse	moos	molded dish or dessert
noix	nwah	nuts
omelette	ahm-a-let	omelet
oeuf	oef	egg
oignon	on-nyohn	onion
petit fours	pet-ee-forz	small iced cakes
poisson	pwah-shoh	fish
pomme de terre	pohm duh tair	potato
potage	po-tazh	soup
poulet	poo lay	chicken
prix fixe	pree-feez	entire meal at one price
ragoût	rah-goo	stew
rôti	roh-tee	roast
riz	ree	rice
soufflé	soo-flay	airy dish made with eggs
soup du jour	soop doo joor	soup of the day
table d′hôte	tabla dote	whole meal at one price
veau	vo	veal
vichyssoise (German)	vee-she-swaz	cold soup
vinaigrette	vee-neh-gret	vinegar dressing

Appendix B

How to Eat Difficult Foods

Artichokes—To properly eat an artichoke, pull one leaf from the heart with your fingers and dip it into the sauce. Place the leaf in your mouth and pull it through your teeth, biting off the soft end. Put the uneaten part on the side of your plate. After eating the leaves, scrape away the thistlelike part in the center with your knife, and eat the heart with your knife and fork.

Asparagus—By reputation it is a finger food, but today it is recommended that you eat it with a fork.

Avocado—Use a fork when the avocado is filled with salad. When served in the shell with salad dressing, use a spoon.

Bacon—Eat bacon with a fork when it is limp. When it is dry and crisp, you may use your fingers.

Bananas—When dining formally, peel the banana, place it on your plate, and cut away one bite at a time with your fork.

Bread and rolls—Pinch off a small portion, buttering it over your plate. Finish eating it before you break off another piece. Don't hold flat bread in the palm of your hand while you butter it. Loaf bread served on a board is sliced with a knife. If you have a biscuit or roll, cut in half, butter, and eat one half at a time.

Candy in frills—Pick up the candy and paper frill lining together from the box or plate without pinching to flavor test it. After you have lifted both from the box or tray, take the piece of candy out of the frill to eat it. Discard the paper frill properly.

Caviar—Made from fish eggs, caviar is an expensive, salty relish. Spread it on a cracker with a knife.

Celery, olives, and other relishes—These may be finger foods, or a toothpick may be provided. You may use a fork, but don't chase an olive around your plate. Use a serving spoon or fork to retrieve items from a communal dish.

Cherry tomatoes—Some people won't eat them for fear of getting a bad one. Unless they are served in a salad, they are a finger food. In a salad cut one with a knife or leave them whole to eat. However, they can squirt if you bite into one, and a bad one can almost send you gagging to the rest room.

Fajitas—This delicious, hot and spicy dish is constructed at the table by the diner and eaten with the hands.

Fried chicken—At a formal dinner it must be eaten with a fork and knife. In someone's home, watch the hostess to see how she eats it. At a picnic or fast-food restaurant, you may use your fingers. Tablecloths usually mean that you should eat the chicken with a knife and fork. Plastic forks and paper plates or boxes call for eating chicken with your fingers.

Clams and oysters—Spear one with the small shellfish fork (or the smallest fork provided). Eat them whole. When they are served as hors d'oeuvres, on a picnic, or in a clam and oyster bar, pick the shell up with your fingers and let the morsel slide into your mouth.

Corn on the cob—Because it is never served at formal meals, it may be eaten with the fingers by grasping each end or by holding the corn holder inserted in the ends. Butter and season a small portion at a time. Don't eat up and down the row like a mowing machine.

Crab legs—A cracking instrument for seafood should be provided. After the claws are cracked, the shells are pulled apart with the fingers and the meat is pulled out with the small oyster fork. This is dipped into melted butter before eating. The small claws are pulled from the body with the fingers and then put in the mouth with the body end of the claws between the teeth so that the meat can be extracted by chewing. Be careful not to make a sucking noise as you chew on these tasty bits. If no crackers or implements are provided, use your hands. Soft-shell crabs are considered a delicacy and are eaten with a knife and fork. You may remove the black vein with your knife and fork and lay it on the plate.

Dips—Whether you are dipping chips or raw vegetables into a dip dish, transfer the food to your buffet plate if you have one. If you have only a napkin, hold the napkin under it while you retreat from the communal bowl before placing the chip in your mouth. Never transfer it directly to your mouth from the communal bowl. You should never appear to be eating from the dip dish. Never take a bite from a chip or vegetable and then put it back into the dip mixture to dip it again. Never fish around for a submerged chip with your fingers. If fresh vegetables are passed at the table, place them on your bread-and-butter plate, salad plate, or on the edge of whatever plate you have. Never eat from the serving dish or plate.

Egg cups—Tap around the top of the egg with a knife. Lift off the top and put it on the serving plate. Season the egg in the cup and eat it from the cup with a spoon.

Finger bowls—You will sometimes detect a fragrance or see flower petals floating. Lemon wedges are appropriate in finger bowls only after a lobster feast. If the waiter or hostess brings a finger bowl before dessert, place the spoon to the right and the fork to the left of your plate. Lift the finger bowl and its doily, placing them to the left of your place setting. The dessert will then be served on the plate. After everyone finishes with dessert, dip your fingertips in the water and dry them on your napkin—one hand at a time. If the finger bowl arrives without utensils, it means "use me when everyone has a bowl." Believe it or not, until the nineteenth century it was the custom to rinse out the mouth and spit the water back into the bowl.

Fish—Baked fish is eaten with a fish knife and fish fork if they are available. The rules for fried chicken apply to fried fish.

Garnishes—Parsley, dill, watercress, mint, and other garnishments may be eaten with the fork as part of the dish of food, if you wish.

Grapes—Cut or break off a small bunch from the larger bunch and pluck one grape at a time, thus preserving the beauty of the larger bunch.

Grapefruit—Use a spoon, preferably a serrated one. Do not squeeze the juice into a spoon except at home.

Gravy—Ladle gravy from the gravy boat. Don't pour it. If you like bread soaked in gravy, you may pinch off a small piece of bread and put it in the gravy on your plate and eat it with your fork. Long ago that custom was called "sopping the gravy." People sopped with their fingers and did so only at home.

Hors d'oeuvres—We often call hors d'oeuvres *appetizers*. They have not always been served first. Once they were side dishes. Hors d'oeuvres literally means outside the works. They are eaten with the fingers.

Iced tea and lemon—Cover the lemon wedge with one hand, squeezing it with your other hand. You may choose to put the wedge in your glass and use the iced teaspoon to force the lemon juice out of the lemon in the bottom of the glass, or you may pierce the lemon wedge with your clean fork. If you do not care for lemon, place it on the small dish beneath the iced tea glass or on some other plate in your service. Never leave any garnishment on the rim of your glass.

Lemon and fish—A lemon squeeze is a lemon wedge wrapped in cheese cloth to prevent squirting juice on someone when you squeeze your lemon. Without a lemon squeeze, use the same method you used with the iced tea. Press out the juice onto the fish with your right hand, while covering the wedge of lemon and your right hand with your left hand.

When great banquets used to begin with processions into the hall, all knives had to be sheathed until carving began. The points of formal dinner-table knives in the West became rounded after 1669, when the French king banned pointed knives at the table, ostensibly in order to discourage the use of them for the picking of teeth.[1]

—Margaret Visser, *The Rituals of Dinner*

Lobster—Unless the claws have been cracked thoroughly before the lobster is brought to you, you will need a nutcracker. To help pull meat from the claws, use a small seafood fork, to get the large pieces of meat from the large claws and the tail and body cavities. You may use a knife to cut them into bite-sized pieces.

Holding the body of the lobster on the plate with your left hand, twist off the claws with your right hand and lay them on the plate. Again holding the lobster steady, lift up the tail meat with your fork. Cut it into manageable segments with your knife. Using your fork, dip a small bite into melted butter. If the lobster is served cold, dip it in mayonnaise. Break off the small claws and quietly suck out the meat. Crack the big claws and extract small segments of the meat with a seafood fork. Dip that bite and put all of it at once into your mouth. With a seafood fork, pick out the meat in the body. Real lobster lovers unhinge the back and open the body of the lobster to extract the remaining sweet morsels.

In the Middle Ages only the nobility had special food knives, which they took with them when traveling: hosts were not usually expected to provide cutlery for dinner guests. To this day in parts of France, men carry with them their own personal folding knives, which they take out of their pockets and use for preference at intimate gathers for dinner.[2]

—Margaret Visser, *The Rituals of Dinner*

Meat—Cut one or two bites at a time. Otherwise the food will get cold quickly, and the plate will look messy.

Melons—Diced melons and cantaloupes are eaten with a spoon.

Oranges—To peel one, cut several slits in the skin from top to bottom around the orange and peel off each section of the skin. Then separate the orange sections, remove the seeds with your fingers, and bite off a small portion of the section of the orange. Whole, unpeeled oranges are not served at a formal meal.

Potatoes—Do not unwrap the foil jacket of a baked potato. Cut a slit in the wrapping and eat the potato with a fork. Garnish a small portion at a time. Don't stir it up into a gooey mess. Put more garnishment as needed. When the butter and sour cream are passed, put a dollop onto your plate with your knife, transferring it to your potato after you pass the dish to the person on your right. You may cut the skin with knife and fork and eat it if you like. Halve French fries with a fork and eat one-half at a time. Chips and shoestring potatoes are eaten with your fingers.

Pickles—Served with a sandwich, pickles are eaten with the fingers. When served with meat, a fork is used.

Pizza—It is a most informal food. You may eat it with a fork, or you may hold a slice with your fingers and nibble from a piece. Don't stuff your mouth.

Salad—You may cut the lettuce with your knife and fork. Afterward, save your knife by placing it on another plate in front of you.

Salt and pepper—Always taste food before seasoning it with salt and pepper or risk offending the hostess's culinary skills and appearing to be impulsive and suspicious. Always pass the salt and pepper shakers together and placing them on the table. Don't pass them from your hands to someone else's hands.

Sandwiches—Cold sandwiches are eaten as finger food. Hot, open-faced sandwiches served on a plate are eaten with a knife and fork. An example of an open-faced sandwich might be hot roast beef on bread served with gravy. Hamburgers and hotdogs are eaten with the hands.

Sauces—You may dip a forkful of food at a time into the sauce on your plate.

Shish kebab—Hold the meat-filled spear in one hand and your fork in the other hand against the handle of the spear. As you pull the spear, push the food off with your fork onto your plate. Eat each piece with your fork, cutting it with your knife if necessary.

Shrimp cocktail—In a tall seafood dish, do not cut the shrimp with your knife. Spearing it with your fork, you may bite into a large shrimp. Cutting it with the edge of your fork is preferable. You may use your left hand to hold the compote steady at the base of the stem. Shrimp in shrimp cocktail is one of the few foods you can bite from while it is still on the fork.

Sorbet—Served immediately before the entrée to cleanse the pallet, it is made of frozen fruit juices. It should never contain milk, as sherbet does. Milk coats the mouth.

Soup—Soup bowls, cups, and even soup plates should have a plate beneath them. Anytime you put down the soupspoon, always place it on the plate, not in the bowl or cup.

When you have a large, shallow soup plate with a wide rim, you may place the spoon in it rather than on the plate beneath it. The soupspoon handle is low enough to thwart an accident such as bumping the handle and flinging the spoon across the table.

In Germany, it is rude to cut potatoes, pancakes, or dumplings with a knife; it looks as though you think they might be tough, and also these starchy foods are thought of as almost like bread. In Italy you never cut spaghetti.[3]

—Margaret Visser, *The Rituals of Dinner*

Spaghetti and sauce—The proper way to eat pasta is to use your fork in your right hand to wind the spaghetti against the inside rim of your plate. Then quickly bring the bite to your mouth, being careful not to slurp up leftover strands. In casual settings you may wind the spaghetti around the fork in the bowl of a large spoon held in your left hand. This is the only exception to the rule stating that a spoon always belongs in your right hand.

Stewed fruit—Eat it with a spoon. Discreetly deposit any pits into the spoon and back into your bowl.

Tortillas—Tacos are eaten with the fingers. Soft tortillas, such as tamales and enchiladas, are eaten with a fork.

Tortilla Wraps—Warm and cold tortilla wraps are usually wrapped in paper and may be eaten with your hands. Leave the paper around the bottom of the wrap as you eat it. If you prefer, remove the paper, lay the food on a plate, and eat it with a knife and fork.

Toothpicks in hor d'oeuvres—Collect them in your paper napkin until you can find a wastebasket or a small plate near the hors d'oeuvres tray for the used picks. Never put them back on the serving platter. Never leave one in your mouth. Toothpicks in club sandwiches should be placed near the edge of your plate before eating the sandwich.

Watermelon—Eat with a fork. When it is cut into small pieces and served in a dish, eat it with a spoon. Seeds should be dropped into your spoon or into your hand if you are eating with a fork.

Zucchini—Eat this vegetable with a fork.

Appendix C

Tipping

The tip is supposed to be a reward for service performed. It also supplements an employee's income (less than minimum wage). The tip comes from an innkeeper's sign "To Insure Promptness." There was a box just inside the establishment. When customers deposited a few coins, they received their drinks or food faster.[1]

Automobile Valet—$2.00 unless you are in an expensive, upscale restaurant or hotel; then the tip should be $3.00.

Barbers—Tip 15 to 20 percent of the bill, but never less than $1.00.

Bellman—Tip $1.00 per bag. If you require special service, tip an extra $5.00.

Busboy—A tip is unnecessary. They are usually compensated by a part of the tip you leave for the waiter.

Cafeteria—Tip only if the waiter carries your tray.

Captain/headwaiter—Tip 5 percent of the bill if you see a separate box on the bill (15 to 20 percent to the waiter). If the captain moves tables together or does some other special service for you, tip him $5.00 with a handshake upon leaving.

Carwash attendant—Look for a tip box. Tip $.50 to $1.00.

Caterer—The tip is usually included in the service charges. If not, tip 15 percent of the catering charge in one lump sum to the manager who will divide it with the helpers.

Hotel maid—Tip $1.00 for each night. Place the money in an envelope marked "maid" on the last day.

Coatroom attendant—Tip $1.00 if there is no fixed charge; otherwise, round up to the next dollar.

Shuttle service—A tip is not necessary unless the driver helps you with your bags. Tip $2.00.

Hotel concierge—Tip $5.00 to $20.00 upon your arrival or $5.00 to $50.00 on your departure, depending on any special services performed for you, such as making air reservations, obtaining choice theater tickets or dinner reservations at the last minute.

Deliveries—Tip $.50 to $1.00.

Doorman—Always tip $.50 to $1.00 to anyone for summoning a taxi for you. A tip to someone opening a door for you is unnecessary.

Facial, makeup, waxing, or other personal service—Fifteen percent of the fee.

Fishing and hunting guides—Tip $5.00 for a one-day trip; $10.00 for a weekend; $20.00 and up for a week.

Flight attendants—Do not tip.

Golf caddies—Tip 15 to 20 percent of the greens fees for eighteen holes.

Golf pro—No tip. You may give a gift at Christmas.

Hair stylists—Do not tip the owner; otherwise tip 10 to 15 percent of the bill.

Health and fitness clubs—Locker room attendants may have a basket displayed. $1.00 is the usual tip.

Hospital staff—Do not tip. You may present a gift upon departure to thank a nurse or aide.

Instructor—Ski, tennis, or golf trainers are not usually tipped. Gifts are proper.

Mairtre d'hotel—Tip $5.00 to $15.00 in a handshake for any special services performed for you.

Manicurist/pedicurist—Tip $2.00 for simple manicures; otherwise, 15–20 percent of the fee.

Masseuse or masseur—Tip 20 percent of the cost of the massage.

Onboard ships—Discuss tips with your travel agent or cruise director. Never tip a ship's officers or purser.

Parking attendant/valet—Tip $1.00 to $2.00 in small town or mid-size cities, $2.00 to $3.00 in large cities.

Personal trainers and exercise instructors—No tip. You may give a gift at Christmas.

Pool lifeguards—No tip.

Redcaps (train porters)—Tip $1.00 per bag or whatever is posted.

Shampoo person—Tip $1.00 to $3.00 depending on the amount of service provided.

Shoe shine—Tip $.50 to $1.00.

Skycaps—For curbside service, tip $1.00 per bag.

Taxi—Tip 15 percent of fare. Minimum tip is $.50.

Tennis pro—No tip. You may give a Christmas present.

Waiter for room service—Tip 15 percent of the bill. The room service charge on the tab goes to the hotel.

Waiter/waitress—Tip 15 to 20 percent of the bill. If you are unhappy with the service, reduce the tip to 10 percent. You may tactfully tell the servers why you were not pleased. If the food is poorly prepared, tell the manager so he can alert the cooks.

Washroom attendant—Usually a coin dish is present. Leave $.50. In a luxury hotel, leave $1.00. Before going to the powder room, be sure you have some change.[2]

Appendix D

Questions and Answers

Dining

Q. Can you eat fried chicken with your fingers?

A. It depends on where you are. If you are in someone's home, watch the hostess and eat your chicken the same way she does. Generally, if there is a tablecloth on the table, the meal is formal enough for a knife and fork. In a fast-food place or on a picnic, you may eat with your fingers.

Q. Is it all right to tuck my napkin in the collar of my shirt?

A. No. It looks juvenile. However, in restaurants that serve barbecue ribs or lobster, you are often given a bib because these things are so messy.

Q. What if I have to sneeze or cough at the table?

A. You should turn your head to one side and cough or sneeze into your napkin. Usually, there is not time enough to grab a handkerchief. You should never blow your nose in your napkin.

Q. What if I have to burp?

A. If you must, be sure to close your mouth to muffle the sound, and then quietly say, "Excuse me."

> Belch near no man's face with a corrupt fumosity;
> Turn from such occasion, it is a stinking ventosity.
> —Hugh Rhodes, *Boke of Nurture*

Q. What is the difference in American and Continental style eating?

A. In American style eating if you are right-handed, you should hold your fork in your left hand and the knife in your right hand to cut your food, then switch the fork to the right hand to eat what you have cut. In Continental style the knife remains in the right hand and the fork remains in the left hand. The fork is kept tines down and food is placed on the back of the fork and lifted to your mouth.

> *The first modern fork . . . is mentioned as having been used in the eleventh century by the wife the Venetian Doge (in Italy). Since they resembled the devil's pitchfork, forks were not seen again until 1391, but it was in the 1500s before they were commonly used for eating because they were considered obscene by the clergy.*[1]
>
> —Margaret Visser, *The Rituals of Dinner*

Q. If American and Continental styles are both acceptable today, can I switch back and forth between the two styles? For instance, can I eat my meat using the Continental style and then eat my vegetables American style, by switching my fork to the right hand?

A. Probably not. Try to be consistent throughout the meal.

Q. Is it good etiquette to invite my boss to lunch or dinner?

A. No. It is up to him or her to extend the invitation.

Q. What does *tip* stand for?

A. It is an acronym for "To Insure Promptness."

Q. When is it necessary to reciprocate an invitation?

A. Parties in private homes such as luncheons or dinner parties usually require a return invitation, unless your boss is entertaining.

Q. I don't drink alcoholic beverages. Must I decline cocktail party invitations?

A. Not necessarily. *Emily Post on Entertaining* says that good hostesses have soft drinks of some kind available. Say, "No, thank you" to an alcoholic drink and ask for a soft drink instead.[2]

Q. Is it all right to take your beverage to the dining room when the hostess announces that dinner is served?

A. You may take your beverage with you only if the hostess suggests that you do.

Q. If there are no place cards, how do I know where to sit?

A. The hostess will usually tell you where she would like everyone to sit.

Q. Where are the honored guests seated at a dinner party?

A. The female guest of honor sits on the host's right and the male guest of honor sits on the hostess' right.

Q. Is it proper to be seated as soon as you find your place card on the table?

A. No, remain standing until everyone is standing at his or her chair. Ladies, including the hostess, are seated by the men, who then take their seats.

Q. Which lady does a man help with her chair? The one on his right or left?

A. Men hold chairs for the women on their right and those on their left if there is no one else to do it.

Q. When dishes are passed around a dining table, which direction should they go?

A. Serving dishes should be passed counterclockwise, or from left to right. It is less awkward to help yourself from your left side.

Q. If you request a dish during the course of a meal, does it still have to be passed counterclockwise to reach you?

A. No. The dish is passed the shortest way possible to the one who requested it.

Q. What do I do when I am offered food at the table that I don't like or to which I am allergic?

A. Either take nothing and pass the dish, or take a little and say nothing, eating what you can or pretending to eat it. If you are offered refreshments in another setting other than the dining room, you properly say, "No, thank you" or "I don't care for any."

Q. Is it acceptable to ask for a second helping at the dinner table?

A. No, it is not proper at a formal dinner, but you may ask at an informal or family gathering. Any time second helpings are offered, you may or may not accept.

Q. Should I turn my glass or cup upside down to indicate that I don't care for any of whatever beverage is being served?

A. No. Simply say, "No, thank you" to the server.

Q. Is it all right to push my plate away to show that I am through eating?

A. No. The signal of your flatware in a parallel position across the plate lets everyone know you are finished. (see illustration on page 118)

Q. When you are offered coffee after dinner, is it all right to ask if it is decaffeinated?

A. Yes. But don't ask for another type of beverage such as tea, unless it is offered.

Q. Should I refold my napkin when I finish eating?

A. No. Lay it flat as you put it on the table beside your place setting after your hostess has placed her napkin on the table signaling that the meal is over.

Q. What is the large plate called that is placed on the table in which the other dishes are served?

A. A charger or service plate. You never eat directly from it. It serves as a resting place for various courses.

Q. How do I know which is my butter plate and which is my salad plate if there are two small plates on the table?

A. The bread-and-butter plate is smaller and is placed above the forks while the salad plate is placed to the left of the forks if it is served with the entrée and not as a separate course. Remember that the words *bread* and *butter* have *b*s in them, and the bread-and-butter plate goes above (another word with *b* in it) the forks.

Q. What is a saltcellar and how is it used?

A. A saltcellar is a small bowl used for serving salt. It usually has a tiny silver spoon. Each guest will have a saltcellar in front of him or her for individual use.

Q. Is it all right to season my food before I begin eating?

A. It is usually considered an insult to the cook to season food before tasting it.

Q. How do I know which glass is the water glass when there are several glasses above my knives?

A. The water glass is always the one on the inside nearest the center of your place setting.

Q. When I sit down to an array of flatware, how do I know what to choose first?

A. You always begin from the outside and move inward. If soup is the first course, there will be a soup spoon on the far right of your place setting.

Q. What is the difference between a tea and a reception?

A. There is usually a receiving line for the guest of honor at receptions. The food served is more substantial than that served at afternoon teas.

Q. What should I do with toothpicks, bones, shrimp tails, etc. during a party or buffet when there are no plates on which to leave them?

A. Place them in a paper napkin held in your hand. If you don't see a receptacle for such things, ask your hostess where you might find one.

Q. What is a brunch?

A. It is a combination of breakfast and lunch, held closer to the lunch hour than in the early morning. Brunches are usually rather informal. Food may even be arranged on a buffet table.

Q. What if I am invited to someone's private club for dinner or a round of golf? How can I reciprocate if I don't belong to a club?

A. You do not have to respond in kind. You can invite the other person to a public golf course, your home for dinner, or a nice restaurant. You may suggest any event or activity you think he or she might enjoy.

Q. Is it proper for me to serve myself before passing a dish to the person beside me?

A. Yes. You may do so without comment, or you can say, "You won't mind if I serve myself first." If the group is large, you may never see the dish again.

Q. I know that toothpicks should not be used in public, but what about using my fingers if I have a problem tooth?

A. It is not proper to use a toothpick or to use your fingers to pick at your teeth. You must excuse yourself to the rest room if the food particle is particularly bothersome.

Introductions

Q. Why is a first impression so important?

A. When people see us for the first time, many form an instant assessment of us in the first ten to fifteen seconds, and it takes many future encounters to change that impression. Ninety-three percent of the impression we make on others is based on what they see.

Q. What should I do if I see someone approaching whom I should introduce, but I can't remember his or her name?

A. First, you should not plan to ignore the effort to make the introduction. There are several things you can try to refresh your memory of the forgotten name. (1) You can reintroduce yourself as the person approaches you, hoping the other person will reintroduce himself or herself. (2) You can look at the person who just approached and say, "I'd like you to meet Bob Larson" and hope the new person will state his name. (3) If all else fails, simply admit that your mind has gone blank and ask the person to give you the name again. Doing so is far kinder than ignoring the introduction.

Q. How should I introduce someone whose title is doctor?

A. Say, "This is my brother, Dr. Sam Houser." The new acquaintance should be given enough information such as a title in order to address the person properly.

Q. How do I decide when or if I should call people by their first name?

A. A younger person should use the last name and wait for an older person to tell him or her to use the first name.

Q. What can I do to keep someone from giving me the "fish" handshake?

A. Few things are more uncomfortable than a limp handshake. To prevent one, grasp the other person's hand with strength and vigor. You can even press down with your thumb, hoping to encourage a better handshake.

Q. How should I shake hands with someone who puts out his or her left hand?

A. Grasp the extended hand from the side with your right hand.

Q. Is it proper to correct my name when I am incorrectly introduced?

A. Yes, wait until the introduction is finished and then say, "It's John."

Conversation

Q. How close is too close when you stand to talk with someone? I'm uncomfortable standing close to someone face-to-face.

A. The distance between two people should be about eighteen inches or an arm's length away.

Q. In making conversation with someone, what subjects should I avoid?

A. Avoid talking about your own health and that of others, except in a general way. For instance, "I've recovered nicely from my surgery. Thank you for asking." Also avoid controversial issues such as politics that could evoke an emotional reaction from the other person and create an argument. Other subjects include a person's age or income, personal misfortunes, ethnic or off-color stories, all gossip, and anything that makes another person feel uncomfortable.

Q. What are some safe and easy conversation topics?

A. People like to talk about themselves. You can ask how the other person and/or his or her family has been doing if you know the person that well. Comment favorably on your surroundings or the occasion that brought you together. Read the newspaper every day for up-to-date news to discuss. Use humor if it is directed toward yourself and not someone else. Listen carefully to what the other person says so that you can respond properly. You may talk about travel or vacations.

Q. What should I do if I am talking to one person and another person walks up and stands nearby?

A. Unless you are in a private conversation, by all means, acknowledge the new person and include him or her in the conversation. If your discussion is truly private, perhaps you should move to a private location.

Q. How can I escape someone who continues to talk on and on?

A. Be polite, wait for a break in the conversation, and say, "I'd really like to hear more about your trip, but I must circulate a little among our class reunion buddies before some of them leave."

The Workplace

Q. Is it all right to hug people in the business world?

A. The Institute of Business Management in Washington says the only thing you should touch on another person is his or her hand or arm. No backslapping or hugging from the front. (You can put an arm around someone from the side.)

Q. What if someone approaches me with a full frontal hug?

A. You can turn to one side and hug shoulder to shoulder, but sometimes it's better to go along with the hug and say nothing.

Q. How soon should I offer my business card to a new acquaintance?

A. After several minutes of conversation. Don't assume that everyone wants or needs your card. Never hand them out indiscriminately.

Q. What about calling people "Honey" or "Sweetheart" in the office?

A. In business, do not use pet or endearing names for either women or men to avoid harassment charges, according to the Institute of Business Management in Washington.

Q. Should I tell a coworker he or she has bad breath?

A. Only if you know him very well. Otherwise, the kindest thing to do is speak to the supervisor who performs the annual evaluation of that employee and let him or her talk to the person about it.

Q. When entering or leaving an elevator, do men stand aside and let the women go first?

A. The person, male or female, closest to the door enters first and holds the door for those following. Upon exiting a crowded elevator those directly in front of the door get off first and make sure the door does not close on someone following.

Q. If I am in a job interview and the prospective employer receives a phone call, what should I do?

A. Rise and ask softly, "Should I wait outside?" If the call is not of a private nature, the employer will likely signal you back to your chair.

Q. What does the term *headhunter* mean?

A. It is a slang expression for an executive recruiter who is retained by a corporation to find qualified candidates for specific positions.

Q. Should I call back after an interview to see if the job has been filled, and how long should I wait?

A. First, write a thank-you note and give it a few days to reach the office of the person who interviewed you. Then you may call to see if the job has been filled. If it hasn't, you may say that you are still interested.

Correspondence

Q. When is it correct to use Ms., Mrs., and Miss?

A. Before the 1970s, we had only Mrs. and Miss. After women began entering the workforce in stronger numbers, Ms. was invented because often you don't know if the woman is married or single. If you are ever in doubt, use Ms. If you know the woman is married and prefers Mrs., use that. After about age 25, most single women use Ms.

Q. How can I make clear that I prefer Mrs. to Ms.?

A. Indicate your preference before your name, as (Mrs.) Lynn Welter.

Q. If I am invited out to a business lunch or dinner, how soon must I write a thank-you note?

A. Write one within twenty-four hours, if possible. Address it to the inviter's office.

Q. Can one ever change an acceptance to a regret regarding an invitation?

A. Acceptable reasons for doing this include illness, death in the family, or a sudden, unavoidable trip.

Q. How do I change my response to an invitation from no to yes?

A. You may call the hostess and explain that the circumstances have changed and ask if you may change your no to yes. If the party is small—a private dinner party, for instance —the hostess will probably have filled your place, and it might embarrass her if you ask to come anyway.

Q. What does "regrets only" mean on an invitation?

A. It means that you reply only if you are unable to go to the function. Do not reply if you plan to attend. If you do not answer the invitation, the host expects you to be there.

Q. How should I address correspondence to a married couple who use different last names?

A. Address the correspondence so that both names appear on the same line: Mr. James Askew and Ms. Mary Markham. (Only married people have their names on the same line with "and" connecting them.)

Q. How should I address correspondence to a female doctor and her husband who is not?

A. Mr. James Marlar and Dr. Ann Marlar.

Q. Is it all right to type my personal correspondence?

A. Only personal letters should be typed. Thank-you notes, invitations, and letters of condolences should be handwritten.

Weddings and Funerals

Q. What about wearing black to a funeral? Is it still expected?

A. Black is still a good color for funerals, but it is no longer necessary unless you are an honorary pallbearer or will be sitting with the family. However, no one should wear bright clothing that would be conspicuous.

Q. May a single person bring a guest to a wedding or party?

A. You may if the invitations reads "and guest."

Q. When the invitation reads "and guest" and you choose to take someone, should you tell the host or hostess your guest's name when you respond?

A. Yes, you should give the name and address so the host may send that person an invitation if he chooses to do so.

Q. How should I dress for a formal daytime wedding?

A. Women guests should wear street-length, dressy dresses. Men should wear a dark suit, white shirt, and a conservative tie.

General Etiquette Questions

Q. What is the difference between manners and etiquette?

A. Etiquette rules are in our head, and manners are in our heart. Etiquette rules tell us what to do, when, and how to do it. Manners make us conscious of the comfort of the other person. In other words, knowing the rules may enable us to recognize a mistake in etiquette the other person makes, but our manners will keep us from saying anything about the rule because it would embarrass the other person. Finally, manners are the application of the rules.

Q. What is the correct way to say the word *etiquette*?

A. It is pronounced et-i-ket. The *q* is pronounced like a *k*. Never say eti-qwet'-tee.

Q. What is the Golden Rule of business?

A. The Golden Rule is the same in any setting. It states *Do unto others as you would have them do unto you.* It comes from the Bible and is the guiding principle for comfortable living in our society.

Q. What is the Platinum Rule?

A. *Do unto others as they would like done unto them.* In other words, consider the personality of the other person. If she is shy and retiring and you are aggressive, don't rush up to her and knock her over with your enthusiasm because that is not what she would like done to her.

Q. What is netiquette?

A. It is a set of rules for behaving properly when you are on-line. In cyberspace you should be as courteous as if you were face-to-face with the other person. Reread everything before sending it out to make sure it is polite and what you really want to say. Check spelling and grammar.

Q. I have been told that men are expected to walk on the side closest to the curb when walking with a woman. Why is that?

A. Long ago men walked near the roadway to protect the woman from splashes of mud from carriage wheels or from the trash thrown out second-story windows. Even though these reasons are no longer valid, the pattern has been established and is still followed.

Telephone

Q. How soon should I instruct my employees to answer the telephone?

A. Answer by the second ring. Approximately 75 to 85 percent of today's business is conducted on the telephone. Consider the telephone a valuable business asset.

Q. How can I politely end a telephone call with someone who keeps on talking when I have work to do?

A. By politely telling that person the truth, that you are busy and will have to continue your conversation at a later time. Or you can say, "I have a report to finish. I'll have to get back to you tomorrow with the answer to your question."

Formal Wear

Q. What do white tie, black tie, formal, semiformal, informal and casual mean?

A. The most formal evening wear is *white tie* which means you wear a white bow tie, a wing collar shirt, and a black tailcoat. For women, a long gown should be worn. Today only official and diplomatic occasions and a rare private ball specify "white tie."

Black tie or *formal* is a tuxedo with a winged-collar shirt and a black bow tie. Jackets may be white in the summer and black the rest of the year. Women usually wear a long dress, but a short, cocktail-length dress is also acceptable.

Semiformal means women wear dresses or nice slacks, and men wear sports shirts and slacks. Neither should wear T-shirts or jeans. Sometimes "semiformal" means dresses for women and suits with ties for the men. If you are in doubt, you may check with the hostess who issued the invitation; or if it is a public gathering, you may ask friends what the local custom is.

Informal or *casual* means just that. Choose something comfortable but neat, pressed, clean, and in good condition. For instance, for a poolside party, you may wear shorts or jeans and a T-shirt.

Gifts

Q. Is it necessary to thank an associate in another company who gives me a gift for the business I brought his way?

A. Yes. Courtesy says that all gifts should be acknowledged, preferably in writing.

■■ ■■ ■■

A View of Manners from Bible Days

Questions and answers abound in Scripture with the greatest answer being Christ the Lord. He is the way, the truth, and the life. By no other name can anyone be saved from eternal separation from God.

Jesus gave us a good example in how we should answer some questions. He showed great humility in His response to Pilate's questioning. He showed that if you are the Messiah, the Son of God, you don't have to prove anything.

Jesus Faces the Governor (Pilate)

Now Jesus stood before the governor. "Are You the King of the Jews?" the governor asked Him. Jesus answered, "You have said it." And while He was being accused by the chief priests and elders, He didn't answer.

Then Pilate said to Him, "Don't You hear how much they are testifying against You?" But He didn't answer him on even one charge, so that the governor was greatly amazed (Matt. 27:11–14).

Prophecy Fulfilled

The events of Matthew 27:11–14 were prophesied in Isaiah. When Scripture is fulfilled, our faith is built up. About seven hundred years before Jesus came, Isaiah prophesied how Jesus would handle such questioning: "He was oppressed and He was afflicted, Yet He did not open His mouth; Like a lamb that is led to slaughter, And like a sheep that is silent before its shearers, So He did not open His mouth" (Isa. 53:7 NASB).

Endnotes

Chapter 1

1. *Margaret Visser, The Rituals of Dinner (New York: Grove Weidenfeld, 1991)*, 25.

2. Ibid., 25.

Chapter 2

1. Barbara Mahany, "Gestures Help You Get to the Gist of Things," *The Arkansas Democrat-Gazette*, 14 August 1997, 2B.

2. *American Health*, September 1990, 34.

3. Howard Muson, "Taking a Stand on Posture," *American Health*, May 1991, 55.

4. Dorothea Johnson, founder and director of The Protocol School of Washington®, www.Psow.com (call toll-free 877-766-3757).

5. Fred H. Wight, *Manners and Customs of Bible Lands* (Chicago: Moody Bible Institute, 1953), 274.

Chapter 4

1. Debra Fine, *The Fine Art of Small Talk*, (Englewood, Colo.: Small Talk Press, 2002), 24.

Chapter 5

1. Linda and Wayne Phillips, *The Concise Guide to Executive Etiquette* (New York: Doubleday, 1990), 159.

2. Ibid., 165.

3. *The Arkansas Democrat-Gazette*, March 1998

4. *The Arkansas Democrat-Gazette*, 1998.

5. John Molloy, *The Woman's Dress for Success* (New York: A Time Warner Company, 1996), 119.

6. Fred H. Wight, *Manners and Customs of Bible Lands*, 92.

7. Ibid.

8. Ibid., 98, 100.

Chapter 6

1. Peggy Post, *Emily Post's Etiquette, 75th Edition* (New York: HarperCollins, 1997), 477–78.

2. Fred H. Wight, *Manners and Customs of Bible Lands*, 135, 137.

Chapter 7

1. *The Arkansas Democrat-Gazette*, August 2001.

2. Dorothea Johnson, founder and director of The Protocol School of Washington®, www.Psow.com, (call toll-free 877-766-3757).

Chapter 8

1. Victor Godinez, "Right Method Can Help Get Applicant's Message Across," *The Dallas Morning News*, 25 November 2001.

2. Ibid.

3. Joyce Lain Kennedy, "Online Résumés Present Pitfalls," *The Dallas Morning News*, 25 November 2001.

4. Hendrix College Career Services, Hendrix College, Conway, Arkansas.

5. Lou Kennedy, *Essential Business Etiquette* (Corpus Christi, Tex.: Palmetto Publishing, 1997), 54.

6. Dorothea Johnson, founder and director, The Protocol School of Washington®, www.Psow.com, (call toll-free 877-766-3757).

7. The Sherwin-Williams Company.

8. Letitia Baldrige, *Complete Guide to Executive Manners* (New York: Rawson Associates, 1985), 339.

9. Fred H. Wight, *Manners and Customs of Bible Lands*, 225–26.

Chapter 9

1. Steven L. Feinberg, ed., *Crane's Blue Book of Stationery* (New York: Doubleday, 1989), 141.

2. Ibid., 5.

3. Ibid., 141.

4. Margaret Visser, *The Rituals of Dinner* (New York: Grove Weidenfeld, 1991), 104.

5. Steven L. Feinberg, ed., *Crane's Blue Book of Stationery*, **need page number**.

6. Peggy Post, *Emily Post's Etiquette, 75th Edition*, 46.

7. Fred H. Wight, *Manners and Customs of Bible Lands*, 62.

Chapter 11

1. *Emily Post's Guests and Hosts* (New York: HarperCollins, 1994), 120.

2. *Focus on the Family Magazine,* May 2002.
3. Fred H. Wight, *Manners and Customs of Bible Lands,* 69.
4. Ibid., 72, 272.

Chapter 12

1. *The Arkansas Democrat-Gazette,* 4 May 2002.
2. *National Etiquette Enterprises Newsletter,* March 1993.
3. Fred H. Wight, *Manners and Customs of Bible Lands,* 294–95.

Chapter 14

1. Fred H. Wight, *Manners and Customs of Bible Lands,* 64, 67, 68.

Chapter 16

1. Peggy Post, *Emily Post's Etiquette, 75th Edition,* 276.

Chapter 18

1. Margaret Visser, *The Rituals of Dinner,* n.p.
2. Ibid., 213.
3. Ibid., 193.
4. Ibid., 257.
5. Walter Scott, "Personality Parade," *Parade Magazine,* 23 June 2002.
6. Margaret Visser, *The Rituals of Dinner,* 258.

Chapter 21

1. Bess McFadden Sanders, The Graces/Gentle-man Company, Pine Bluff, Arkansas.

Appendix B

1. Margaret Visser, *The Rituals of Dinner,* 98.
2. Ibid., 184.
3. Ibid., 186.

Appendix C

1. June Hines Moore, *The Etiquette Advantage* (Nashville: Broadman & Holman Publishers, 1998), 129.
2. Peggy Post, *Emily Post's Etiquette, 75th Edition* and Bess McFadden Sanders of the Graces/Gentle-man Company, Pine Bluff, Arkansas.

Appendix D

1. Margaret Visser, *The Rituals of Dinner,* 335.
2. Emily Post, *Emily Post on Entertaining* (New York: Harper Perennial), 30.

Bibliography

Baldrige, Letitia. *Letitia Baldrige's New Complete Guide to Executive Manners.* New York: Macmillian Publishing Company, 1993.

Blake, Gary, and Bly, Robert W. *The Elements of Business Writing.* New York: Macmillian Publishing Company, 1991.

Cunningham, Chet. *How to Meet People and Make Friends.* Leucadia, Calif.: United Research Publishers, 1992.

Feinberg, Steven L., ed. *Crane's Blue Book of Stationery.* New York: Doubleday, 1989.

Kennedy, Lou. *Essential Business Etiquette.* Corpus Christi, Tex.: Palmetto Publishing, 1997.

Martinet, Jeanne. *The Art of Mingling.* New York: St. Martin's Press, 1992.

Mastering Business Etiquette and Protocol. Alexander, Va.: The National Institute of Business Management, Inc., 1995.

Mercedes, O.P., Sister Mary. *A Book of Courtesy.* New York: HarperCollins Publishers, 2001.

Molloy, John T. *New Women's Dress for Success.* New York: Warner Books, Inc., 1996.

Moore, June Hines. *The Etiquette Advantage.* Nashville: Broadman & Holman Publishers, 1998.

Moore, June Hines. *Manners Made Easy.* Nashville: Broadman & Holman Publishers, 2000.

Phillips, Linda and Wayne. *Executive Etiquette.* New York: Doubleday Dell Publishing Group, Inc., 1990.

Post, Elizabeth L. *Emily Post on Guests and Hosts.* New York: HarperCollins Publishers, 1994.

Post, Elizabeth L., and Coles, Joan M. *Teen Etiquette.* New York: Harper and Row Publishers, Inc., 1986.

Post, Peggy. *Emily Post's Etiquette, 75th Edition.* New York: HarperCollins Publishers, 1997.

Protocol School of Washington®, The. Dorothea Johnson, founder and director. www.Psow.com.

Sanders, Bess McFadden. The Graces/Gentle-Man Company. Pine Bluff, Ark.: McFadden Corporation, 1983.

Visser, Margaret. *The Rituals of Dinner*. New York: Grove Press, Inc., 1991.

Wight, Fred H. *Manners & Customs of Bible Lands*. Chicago: Moody Bible Institute, 1953.

About the Author

June Hines Moore has twenty years of experience in teaching and writing about etiquette. She is a member of International Speakers Association, C.L.A.S.S. (Christian Leaders and Speakers Service), and AWSA (Advanced Writers and Speakers Association). For more information on speaking availability, training workshops, or fees, you may send your E-mail to June Hines Moore at manners@team-national.com. Specific questions on manners or business etiquette cannot be answered individually but are welcome as research for future projects.

Index